62

R.B.W. Nott

1953

From the Author.

MERCY AND
SACRIFICE

MERCY AND SACRIFICE

A Study of the Book of Hosea

by

NORMAN SNAITH, D.D.

SCM PRESS LTD
56 BLOOMSBURY STREET
LONDON

First published September 1953

Printed in Great Britain by
Northumberland Press Limited
Gateshead-on-Tyne

CONTENTS

Preface   7

I. THE FIRST OF THE PROPHETS   9

II. THE MARRIAGE OF HOSEA   27

III. THE ESSENCE OF RELIGION   39

IV. THE SECOND MARRIAGE   70

V. SACRIFICE AND THE PROPHETS   88

VI. THE VALUE OF SACRIFICE   102

Index of Subjects   121

Index of Biblical References   123

PREFACE

THE best known verse in Hosea is Hosea 6.6: 'For I desire mercy and not sacrifice; and the knowledge of God more than burnt offerings.' And so I have taken as my text for this little book on Hosea a variation of the first part of this verse. The scheme of the book is as follows. The Rabbis of old said that Hosea was the first of the prophets. In what sense were they right? Was he the first in time? Was he the first in the particular emphasis which makes his message distinctive? My answer is that he may possibly have been the first in time; he and Amos together were jointly first in their emphasis on the necessity of true religion showing itself in daily life; Hosea was certainly first in his emphasis on 'mercy'. But he said 'mercy and not sacrifice'. What did he mean by this? What was the meaning of 'sacrifice' for the prophets? And what do we mean by 'sacrifice'?

It is my earnest hope that what I have written will help to a fuller understanding of Hosea, both the man and the book. The best use can be made of this study if the many cross-references are carefully tracked down. In this way I hope that it will help to the building up of that faith in Christ without which we are all lost.

NORMAN SNAITH

I

THE FIRST OF THE PROPHETS

ACCORDING to the ancient Jewish traditions, Hosea ben
Beeri was the first of the prophets. By this they did not
mean that he was the first of those prophets who were
associated with the shrines from an early date, that type
from which Amos violently dissociated himself (Amos
7.14), the cultic prophet who shared duties at the local
shrines with the priest. They meant that he was the first
of the canonical prophets, that succession of God-inspired
men who are the glory of God's people Israel. When we
speak or write of the religion of Israel and then draw our
data from the writings ascribed to Hosea, Amos, Isaiah,
Jeremiah and the like, we are really dealing with the
religion of these prophets, of whom Hosea and Amos were
the first. The religion of Israel was very different, as these
prophets themselves have indeed said. The reply of the
people to Jeremiah (44.16-19) is much nearer a description
of the actual state of affairs than we have been prepared
easily to allow. Indeed, Jeremiah himself (44.21) admitted
the truth of it: they and their fathers worshipped the queen
of heaven, probably the Anat of the Ras Shamra (Ugarit)
tablets, and were anything but faithful to Jehovah.

Many of the earlier prophets, the cultic prophets, were
doubtless compromised in this idolatrous worship, if not
whole-heartedly in favour of it. Prophets such as these there

9

had been before Hosea's time, and prophets like these there were after him, but in Hosea and his eighth-century canonical contemporaries, there came new light and truth to the sons of men.

The book 'Hosea' is the first book in the collection of shorter writings known of old to the Jews as 'The Book of the Twelve', or, more shortly, 'The Twelve'. The order of these books was fixed by the Masoretes, or earlier by official sanction, in accordance with what they believed to be the correct historical order, and they deemed Hosea to be the earliest of all. They said (*Baba bathra* 14a) that he would have come first of all the prophets, but since his book was so small, it was placed with the other small volumes in order to prevent its being lost. In the old Greek Version (Septuagint), Hosea does actually come first of all the prophets, even though (since all the Twelve hold firmly together) this involves putting the rest of the so-called 'minor' prophets before Isaiah.

The Rabbis interpreted Hosea 1.2 to mean that the first time God ever spoke through a prophet, it was through Hosea. They said that the phrase in question should read *The beginning of the Lord's speaking was in Hosea*. This interpretation was adopted by Jerome, who owed a great deal to Jewish tradition, especially so far as his last Latin rendering of the Old Testament is concerned, that third Latin Version of his which is the basis of the present-day Vulgate. There is much to be said for this rendering of the Hebrew, because the syntax of the verse makes it difficult to join the phrase to the rest of the verse. Indeed, the Hebrew manuscripts traditionally separate the phrase from what follows. They leave a space after *in Hosea*, and they begin a new paragraph. It is probable that the phrase belongs to the title, and more than likely that, like most of verse 1, it is a later editorial addition, later than the original editorial title which seems to have been: 'The word of the Lord which came to Hosea ben Beeri in the days of Jeroboam ben Joash, king of Israel', followed by (verse 2) 'and the Lord said to Hosea'. All scholars hold that Hosea was a northerner, except recently Ivan Engnell, who has suggested that he was a Judahite or at least had Judahite sympathies. If Hosea was a northerner, it is most unlikely that he, or any other northerner, would have put the names of the Judahite kings first, if indeed he mentioned them at all. The fact that the whole of the Old Testament as we have it now is a southern production, suggests that here in the opening verse of Hosea we have an historical note designed to make southern readers aware of the time of Hosea's prophetic activity, by dating him according to what they believed to be the true succession of Hebrew kings.

But was Hosea actually the first in time of these new prophets?

The modern custom is to make Amos earlier than Hosea by anything up to twenty years. In point of fact there is no paramount reason for dating the beginning of Amos' prophetic ministry much earlier than the year of the death of Jeroboam ben Joash (Jeroboam II) of Israel. The customary early dating (i.e. *c.* 760 B.C.) depends largely upon Amos 8.9 supposing that this is a reference to the solar eclipse of 763 B.C., June 15th, being in the tenth year of Assur-dan III. There is also an additional assumption that if Amos referred to it, it was a recent happening. In that case the earthquake spoken of in the previous verse was a recent happening.

According to Amos 7.10, Amos's appearance at Bethel was during King Jeroboam's reign, but it may easily have been towards the very end of his reign. The problem of the dates of Israelite and Judahite kings is notoriously difficult, and Professor E. R. Thiele has said nothing less than the truth in naming his book (the latest) on the subject *The Mysterious Numbers of the Hebrew Kings*. The numbers are certainly full of mystery in the extreme, and considerable ingenuity is needed in order to make them all fit into anything like a coherent pattern. Scholars of the last thirty years vary between 749 B.C. and 743 B.C. for the year of Jeroboam's death, though Thiele himself advocates a date as early as 753 B.C. It is difficult to bring the year of the king's death any lower than 746 B.C., which is Professor W. F. Albright's estimate. Further, we know (Amos 1.1) that Amos began to preach two years before the devastating earthquake which took place in the reign of King Azariah-Uzziah of Judah, an earthquake which was still spoken of in the somewhat late Zechariah 14.5. (This king's name was probably Azariah. The name Uzziah may have arisen through the accidental omission by a copyist of the letter *r*, as reference to the Hebrew spelling will show.) Azariah's death is variously estimated as having taken place from 747 B.C. to 734 B.C. Professor Albright's estimate is 744 B.C. If the earthquake coincided, as some have said (from Josephus onwards) with the vision described in Isaiah 6 (verse 4: 'the foundations of the thresholds were moved . . . and the house was filled with smoke'), then Amos began to preach in the year 746 B.C. (following Albright's dating), which brings us just within Albright's estimate for the end of Jeroboam's reign. There is no need to insist that Amos began his work as a prophet any earlier than this. Further, this is approximately the date which is usually given for the beginning of Hosea's ministry.

The critical date in near-east politics for this period is the year 745 B.C., the date of the usurpation of the Assyrian throne by Tiglath-pileser III. This meant that the peaceful days were past. By 744 B.C. it was plain to all that the new king was vigorous and adventurous in the extreme, and that everyone between Mesopotamia and the Mediterranean must expect trouble in the near future, and plenty of it. In the first year of his reign he defeated the Armenians who had been the dominant power since the death of Adad-nirari III in 782 B.C. During the next six years he reconquered the territory which the Armenian king Argistis (780-760 B.C.) and his successor had taken from the Assyrians, and continued by conducting various successful campaigns in all directions. Tiglath-pileser was by that time ready for further adventures, and indeed his was the most serious threat that had ever loomed up from the east. In the ninth century, when Shalmaneser III (860-823 B.C.) had marched towards the western sea, there had been a strong Syrian kingdom with its capital at Damascus, and the Syrian king Hadadezer had made the largest contribution of infantry and cavalry to the Aramaean alliance which had held up the Assyrian invader at Karkar by the Orontes. Ahab of Israel had provided most chariots (2,000) and also 10,000 infantry, half as many as Hadadezer. As long as there was a Syrian kingdom of Damascus, however weak, there was a buffer state between Israel and Assyria, and this buffer state could take the first blow and shock of arms. But Shalmaneser's grandson, Adad-nirari III (805-782 B.C.), had marched west and destroyed Damascus in 803 B.C. It took Damascus a long time to recover, so that when Tiglath-pileser was realized to be a war-lord of the same type, Israel had no protection whatever against him, and was naked to the full Assyrian might. The modern parallel is Western Europe with no Germany and a threat from further east.

The closer, therefore, we can date both Hosea and Amos to 745 B.C., the more substance there is in their forebodings for the future and their threats in the immediate present. To a discerning man there was trouble looming ahead as soon as the news came of a usurping king in Assyria, since it would be plain what sort of a king the new monarch would prove to be. After 744 B.C. no true prophet, however patriotic, could hold out the slightest hope for Israel.

It is usually held that the first three chapters of Hosea are earlier than 744 B.C., on the ground that there is hope to be found in them. But this type of statement is surely based upon a misunderstanding, for whilst there is hope in chapter 2, it is hope only for a restoration which follows a return east to the desert. The whole land of Canaan is to be desolate, untilled, subject to the unchecked ravages of the wild beasts (2.12). This, combined with the later references to the wilderness, suggests an exile of the people from their country. There is hope also in chapter 3, but here once again it is a return (verse 5) after a period without king, prince, and the adjuncts of worship which the Israelites came to know in Canaan. There is hope in 6.1-3 also, but once more it is after an interval: 'after two days he will revive us: on the third day he will raise us up, and we shall live before him.' Once more, there is hope in chapter 11.8-9, but again it seems to be hope after a disaster that only just stops short of being final. Verse 9 is difficult to understand, but seems to mean that God will not let loose the full heat of His anger; He will not deliver a second destructive blow upon Israel: 'for I am God and not man: the Holy One in thy midst and no human being' (following the suggestion of Volz, Nowack and Harper, reading *'adam* for *'abo'*, and taking the last word of the verse with the next verse). And the section concludes (if, that is, we are to include verses 10 and 11 in this oracle) with the exiles returning from Egypt and from Assyria like migratory birds coming back again in their season. Chapter 14 speaks of repentance after sad trouble. Israel has fallen, but a time will come when Israel will repent. She will never look for help again to Assyria, nor to Egypt (the reference to 'riding upon horses' needs Isaiah 30.16 to explain it), and never again to idols.

The sum-total of this short review of the book is that nowhere in Hosea is there any hope for Israel before an exile, but only after an exile of 'two-three' days (6.2) or of 'many days' (3.3; if indeed this verse is from eighth-century Hosea: see below, p. 32). This means that so far as certainty of immediate trouble is concerned, there is nothing to choose as regards date between Hosea and Amos. Neither prophet can see any hope for Israel in the face of the coming onslaught from the east. There would be no ground for any one, prophet or no prophet, to assume trouble from the Assyrians until the accession of Tiglath-pileser III. Thus it may well be that the Rabbis were right in their belief that Hosea was the first of these eighth-century prophets. He may possibly have been a year or so earlier than Amos, but there cannot have been much difference between the times of the delivery of their first prophetic words. If indeed Amos did precede Hosea, it is unlikely that there was anything like the gap between them which modern scholars generally assume.

But whether ancient Jewish tradition is right or wrong

in making Hosea the first of the canonical prophets, it is certainly true that in Hosea and Amos we have a new type of prophet and a new type of prophecy. Earlier prophets in Israel were characterized by behaviour of a frenzied type. This has been made clear in English writings by Professor A. R. Johnson in his monograph, *The Cultic Prophet in Ancient Israel* (1944), pp. 17-22. He points out that verbal form used to describe the behaviour of a prophet (*nabi'*) meant, as late as the time of Jeremiah, ' to be frenzied, fanatical, mad' (Jeremiah 29.26), and that it was possible in Jehu's time to describe a prophet as ' that madman' (II Kings 9.11). This latter example by itself would be of no great value, since it might easily be the comment of the soldier concerning ' the cloth' (in those days, a hairy cloak), but there is plenty of support for the idea elsewhere. There are other instances which date as much from the time of writing them down as from the date of the incidents themselves. Saul meets a string of prophets coming down the hillside from the local sanctuary, and he is seized forthwith with their contagious frenzy (I Samuel 10.5-13). A divine power rushed upon him and he ' became another man'. A similar story is told in I Samuel 19.18-24. Both depend upon the belief that Saul was seized by some frenzy and was not in control of his own faculties. The man who is not controlled by his own spirit, must be under the control of some other spirit.

The ancient logic of belief which lies behind this required no particular defence in those far-off days. Given the premises, the conclusion is perfectly logical. It is a mistake to follow M. Lévy-Bruhl in his theory of a pre-logical mentality belonging to ages less scientifically minded than our own. The alternative to his point of view is not ' the

Theory of the Noble Savage', but simply that the difference lies in the different premises of earlier days, rather than in their logical processes. Indeed, there are modern sects whose views concerning divine inspiration are not markedly different from the views of men of a comparatively low stage of culture and knowledge. The argument is: No event takes place without a personal agent. If therefore an event takes place for which there is no apparent human cause, if there takes places an event not directed or controlled by human agency, then clearly the controlling agency must be non-human. The event must have been caused by some *numen*, some spirit, some deity. The man whose own spirit is obviously not controlling his actions or his words, must be under the control of some other spirit. This was held to be the case whatever the type of non-control, whether due to the abnormal psychology of the man himself, or to any artificial stimulation such as music, a frenzied whirling, alcohol, and the rest. What is seen and heard in a vision, a dream or a trance is caused, equally as in the case of other uncontrolled states, by some present *numen*, because there also are cases where sight and hearing are not controlled by the man himself. It is a devastating thought that if only men had invented the 'subconscious mind' early enough in human history, we might never have suspected that there could be any such experience as divine revelation or 'the witness of the spirit'.

This also is the justification of the ancient sacred lot. In our modern times, the result of the casting of a lot is regarded as 'pure chance', that is, as wholly a matter of chance with no element of guidance or control whatever. But to the men of old there was no such thing as chance. If the lot is cast by a holy man ('bring hither the ephod') or in a holy place, then it must be the *numen* of that man or place who caused the lot so to fall. Similarly, it must be the *numen* of the shrine who made those marks on the liver of the animal (cf. the 'text-book' liver tablet found at Gezer) by which the priest declares the word of the god.

But Hosea was different from these earlier prophets of the Canaanite *nabi'* type. There is no evidence that either he or any of his eighth-century contemporaries (Amos, Isaiah, Micah) ever spoke in an ecstasy. The Word of the Lord came to Hosea in full consciousness. He was in complete awareness of what he was doing or saying. The probability is that if a man wished to be recognized as a prophet, he wore a 'hairy mantle' (Zechariah 13.4). This seems to have been the traditional garb of a prophet from Elijah down to John the Baptist. Amos doubtless appeared at the royal shrine of Bethel in his rough shepherd's cloak, so similar to the hairy mantle of the Elijah-Elisha tradition that Amaziah the priest of Bethel easily came to the conclusion that Amos was a prophet of the old traditional type, an identification which Amos indignantly repudiated (Amos 7.14).

The new type of prophet, exemplified first in Hosea and Amos, was then definitely and fully aware of what he said and did. He said it and did it deliberately and out of settled conviction. The man speaks out that which he is certain is God's Word in and through him. It is that of which he is certain in his own heart.

What then is the new test of truth? Wherein lies the authority of the new prophet? The old test was comparatively simple. If the man gibbered and raved, that was sufficient. But the days soon came when some men at least demanded more. Some doubtless were still satisfied with the old ideas and the old tests. The apostle Paul

had difficulties with that kind of thing (I Corinthians 12).
Perhaps it was not all loss, because his difficulties gave us
I Corinthians 13. In Old Testament times, the first stage
of development was that indicated in Deuteronomy 18.22:
'If the thing follow not, nor come to pass, that is the thing
which the Lord hath not spoken.' This may have been
enough in the days when the true character of God was
not known, but there came a time when another test had
to be devised. The thing might come to pass, and yet the
prophet's word might not be the Word of the Lord. And
so, 'if the sign or wonder come to pass' and at the same
time the content of the message be clearly contrary to sound
and true religion (e.g. luring the people away to the worship of other gods), then 'thou shalt not hearken unto the
words of that prophet' (Deuteronomy 13.2-3). The explanation offered is that God is testing the people. It is not
so far denied that the prophet is truly a prophet. Nor is
it denied that his inspiration is of God. If the thing come
to pass, that is, if the sign he shows is satisfactory, he must
be indeed a prophet. But if the content of his message
is obviously wrong, then he must not be followed. Compare I Corinthians 12.3.

It appears therefore that God is, at the stage of
Deuteronomy 13.3, still conceived as putting both true and
false words into the mouths of His prophets. It is still
held that every man who acts as a prophet and gives signs
that can be verified, is inspired by a non-human agent.
Further, in an orthodox henotheistic Israel [Henotheism:
belief in one God without asserting that He is the only
God], there could be no non-human agent other than
Jehovah Himself. The necessary deduction therefore is
that God, for His own purposes, is deceiving either the
hearers (I Kings 22.19-24) or both hearers and prophet

(Jeremiah 20.7). These ideas are parallel to those found in the Qur'an, where God is envisaged in the main as naked power: 'Neither shall my (i.e. Muhammad's) counsel profit you, although I endeavour to counsel you aright, if God shall please to lead you into error' (Sura xi). This is the sentiment of II Samuel 24.1, where God is represented as Himself influencing David to number the people, and then as being angry with David and punishing the people for what David had done at His instigation, against David's own ideas of rightness, fairness and decent conduct generally (verse 17). But in the parallel passage in I Chronicles 21.1 a noteworthy change has been made. It is the Satan, the Adversary, who tempts David into wrong action. Whilst the idea of the Adversary raises problems of its own, we have at least this consolation, that it was recognized by, say, the fourth century B.C. that God cannot, because of His very nature, deliberately lead men into sin or tempt them into wrong action for any reason whatsoever.

What then is the new test of divine guidance and inspiration? Abnormal behaviour is no guarantee. The fulfilment of signs is no guarantee. To say that the message must be tested by what is already known is only partially satisfactory, since the full adoption of this criterion would strangle at birth any revelation of a new type. Such strangling has taken place more than once, and indeed is the usual fate of prophets (Luke 4.24, 13.34, 16.31). Where organized Christianity has gone astray and committed what we now see to be sins against the Holy Spirit, it has largely been by the application of this test of orthodoxy. It constitutes not only the safety of sound religion, but its greatest danger and the source of its more frequent blindness. Supposing that a man speaks and acts according to that of which he is certain in his own heart, how can he be sure that this is the guidance of God and not his own spirit, especially when the 'authorities' of the day desire to silence him? How can we distinguish between true and false prophets, when so far as inner conviction is concerned, both groups are certain and there is nothing, from that point of view, to choose between them?

The answer to these questions can perhaps best be learned from the experience of Jeremiah, a man who in many ways was Hosea's heir and lineal successor as a prophet.

The prophet Jeremiah was always conscious of his call to be a prophet. He said that God knew him whilst still he was unborn, and that he was sanctified to be a prophet before his birth (Jeremiah 1.5). He never knew a time, that is, when he was not conscious of the call to be a prophet. He started his prophetic ministry in his youth, probably in his early twenties, but he made two mistakes, and these two mistakes were probably his first two attempts at prophecy. It is generally agreed, though there are those who differ, that the vision of the bubbling, overheated cauldron of chapter 1 concerns the invasion of the Scythians who burst through the Cilician Gates about 626 B.C., and swept down the Mediterranean coastlands (the Levant). Jeremiah apparently thought that they would capture Jerusalem and set up their thrones in its gateways, the traditional site for judgements delivered by king and conqueror. But he was wrong. The Scythians were defeated by the Pharaoh Psamtik I in a two-day battle near Ascalon and wiped out. Jeremiah was doubtless right on the main issue, that Jerusalem was ripe for punishment, but he was wrong in supposing that the Scythians were the 'rod of the Lord's anger'. The city was to have yet another chance of repentance under the reforms of the good king Josiah, and ultimately Babylon was to be the Lord's rod for Jerusalem.

Jeremiah's second error was in connection with the Deuteronomic reforms under King Josiah. At first he was in favour of these reforms. Apart from the contents of Jeremiah 11.1-8, there is the evidence of the violent and murderous hostility of Jeremiah's own family at Anathoth (11.21-23). If these priests of Anathoth were, as is usually supposed, the descendants of Abiathar, sole survivor of the massacre at Nob, descendant (as is usually supposed) of the House of Eli, ancient guardians of the Ark (I Samuel 2.27-28), then their hostility to Jeremiah finds a ready explanation. He was supporting the Zadokite priesthood of Jerusalem, who had become, since Solomon's time, priests of that Ark which originally was the peculiar care of the family of Eli. But Jeremiah 8.8 shows an antagonism to the priestly scribes of Jerusalem who were using the reform movement for their own aggrandizement and twisting the zeal of the young king to their profit (II Kings 23.9). Jeremiah had been wrong again, because the reforms were directed, not, as he had hoped, to the revival of true religion throughout the land, but to the exaltation of the Zadokite priesthood of Jerusalem and the elimination of the priests in every other succession. Only those priests who were in close alliance with king and state were permitted to continue to function.

And so, after his second failure, there comes a long silence on the part of the young prophet. 'O Lord, thou hast deceived me, and I was deceived: thou art stronger than I, and hast prevailed: I am become a laughing-stock all the day, every one mocketh me . . . and if I say, I will not make mention of him, nor speak any more in his name . . .' (Jeremiah 20.7-9). But the prophet could not remain silent, because, as the passage continues, ' there is in my heart as it were a burning fire shut up in my bones, and I am weary with forbearing, and I cannot contain'.

What had happened to Jeremiah in the meantime? Afterwards, his messages were invariably sound and true. Not only did he say what eventually came to pass, but his messages satisfied the test of sound religion.   At least, we now can see that they satisfied this latter test, just as Judah saw it in the experiences of the Exile; but his contemporaries almost without exception could not see it.   Jeremiah did speak in the Name of the Lord, and it was in truth the Word of the Lord that he spoke.   How did this come about?   The answer is to be found in Jeremiah's enforced personal knowledge of God.

Jeremiah, more than any other Old Testament personage of whom we have anything like sufficient knowledge to judge, was a man made for fellowship and friendship. At the same time he was forced by his convictions to do things and to say the very things which were most calculated to isolate him from everybody else.   This was all the more serious for him because of his nature.   There are some men who can go forward bravely and courageously even though all the world is against them.   It is more than likely, for instance, that Athanasius was far from worried when all the world was against him; he probably enjoyed the situation.   But there are others who are much troubled by such isolation, who immediately become introspective, wondering and worrying whether after all they have done and said what is right.   Jeremiah was of this type.   It was far from a pleasure to him to stand alone; it was, in fact, a very great burden to him and a matter of great distress. But he had to follow the light he had, even though it led him to take a course of action which made even his own relations his bitter enemies. He believed that it was God's will that he should be both wifeless and childless, and yet he was a man who could express himself in terms such as we find in Jeremiah 31.20. It was his duty to speak of the coming destruction of his country and to advise submission to the enemy power, and yet this man was at least as great a lover of his country and his countryside as any of those who maligned him as being unpatriotic and urged if necessary a last-ditch resistance against the foe.

Out of all this tribulation and loneliness, this man Jeremiah was driven to seek and to find a fellowship with God such as no man had known before. He realized the possibility of a direct knowledge of God on the part of the individual. The result was that not only was he able to say that the true and new covenant involved the writing of the law on the heart of every man, but also he was able to say this on the grounds that God had written His law on Jeremiah's own heart. And so, when, after his long silence, Jeremiah spoke once more of that which was embedded deep in his own heart, this message was in very truth the Word of God in a way in which it had not before been so for him. Here is the new test of the prophet and the solution of the problem of certainty. The prophet must indeed speak of that which he is certain in his own heart, but the extent to which this inner certainty coincides with the Word of God depends upon the extent to which the prophet has come to know God in his own inner experience. This inner conviction is paramount over everything else, but a man must be very certain that it arises truly from the Indwelling God. A man must follow the light that is in him, but he must seek out every means of making sure that this light is the Light of the World.

Mostly the Word of God to each man will agree with what the whole fellowship of believers understands by the Word of God, but not always and not necessarily. In the Old Testament, it is generally the case that the true prophet speaks what is by no means acceptable to the general body of believers. It is a case of Scylla and Charybdis. The individual may be confusing the Holy Spirit with his own spirit. The group may be confusing the Will of God with conservatism and group-mindedness. It may be more concerned with preserving the group as it is than in listening for the Word of the living God. Let every man follow the light within him, but let him make sure he is truly instructed in the Way, and let him remember the Judgement Day when the secrets of all hearts shall be revealed, ' and each man's work shall be made manifest'.

We have thus in Hosea and Amos a new type of prophet, one who speaks in full conscious control of his faculties. The Spirit-control which is essential in all prophecy, is to be found in this type of prophet within the man, at the centre and core of his being, behind all his thinking and at the roots of his consciousness. We have used the experience of Jeremiah in order to attempt an explanation of how this new type of prophecy came into existence. The experience of Jeremiah helps us here because he was following the path blazed by Hosea. In this matter of individual personal experience of God, Hosea was the pioneer of a newer prophecy than he ever realized. Hosea found out that religion primarily is a matter of relationship with God, but he continued to think in terms of the relationship of Israel as a whole to God. With him the relationship was that of the nation, of the group. In Jeremiah we have the further stage, where the relationship must be that of the individual with God. This primary personal relationship issues in right conduct amongst other 'fruits', but the fundamental and the starting-point for religion is in this personal realm.

This brings us to the consideration of Hosea's marriage, since it was his experience of a broken-down marriage which led him to find the new paths which God was opening before him.

II

THE MARRIAGE OF HOSEA

THE CONTENTS of the first three chapters of the Book
of Hosea have given rise to unceasing discussion. Did
Hosea really marry Gomer-bath-Diblaim, or is it all allegory from start to finish? If he did actually marry her,
then what sort of a woman was she when he married her?
Was she already a harlot, or did these tendencies show
themselves later, either before the birth of the first child,
or before the birth of the second child? Did God really
command this prophet to marry a woman who was a
harlot, or, what amounts to the same thing from a moral
point of view, a woman who presumably God knew was
a harlot in the making? Is the woman of chapter 3 the
same woman as the Gomer-bath-Diblaim of chapter 1, or
are they separate and distinct persons, the second of whom
was undoubtedly a harlot when the prophet found her,
whatever Gomer-bath-Diblaim may have been?

In the first place, the three separate chapters in the
Hebrew text (in the English text the three sections are
1.2-9, 1.10-2.23, 3.1-5) belong to three separate literary traditions. Section 1 (i.e. 1.2-9) is biographical; section 2 (1.10-
2.23) is oracular; section 3 (i.e. chapter 3) is autobiographical.
The second section from 2.2-2.23 (the first part, 1.10-2.1, is
generally agreed to be from a later hand) is definitely in
verse, but the same cannot be said of chapter 1 and chapter

3. Attempts have been made to find some kind of rhythmical pattern in sections 1 and 3, but a glance at the way
in which the sections are set out in the third edition of
Kittel's *Biblia Hebraica* shows how little can be achieved
in this way. It is much more reasonable to suppose that
sections 1 and 3 (i.e. chapters 1 and 3 apart from the last
two verses of chapter 1) are in prose, especially since those
lines in chapter 1 which most nearly approach verse form
are confined to verse 7, which is agreed on other grounds to
be a later interpolation.

These three different types of writing in the prophets
were pointed out by Professor Mowinckel in 1914 in his
study of the composition of the Book of Jeremiah. First,
there is Type A, which comprises the oracular utterances
of the prophet and is in poetic form. Hosea 2.2-23 is of
this type. Second, there is Type B, which is biographical
and is in prose. Hosea 1 is of this type. Third, there is
Type C, which is autobiographical in form and is in prose.
Hosea 3 is of this type. Further details of these types
can be found in Professor T. H. Robinson's *Prophecy and
the Prophets in Ancient Israel*, first published in 1923, and
also in his article entitled 'Higher Criticism and the
Prophets' in the *Expository Times*, February 1939. Type
A, oracular sayings by the prophet himself, were probably
handed on orally by those that heard them, and later,
perhaps when the prophet was dead, collected into small
collections and ultimately written down. Perhaps some of
these oracles, usually quite short, were dictated by the
prophet himself and faithfully written down by some faithful 'Baruch'. Type B, biographical prose, would be more
subject to variation, and it would be easier here than in the
case of Type A for sayings to be added by some devoted
disciple who thought them to be worthy of his master,

even though the master may not have been responsible
for them. This tendency would explain the interpolation
in chapter 1, where verse 7 seems to belong to other times
and to another prophet, even though it has been cast into
a form similar to that of its present context. The general
opinion of present-day scholars is that additions are more
likely to be made in Type B than in Type C, so that they
think that, other things being equal, Type B is more
reliable than Type C. This, however, is not what Professor
Mowinckel thought. He was of the opinion that Type C
was the latest type to be gathered together and written
down. We shall return to this point later. Meanwhile,
in any case, we have three chapters belonging to three
different literary traditions, originally belonging to three
different collections, with the common theme of a marriage
that has broken down.

In the second place, if we are to take the three chapters
as reflecting in every detail an original story, it is evident
that the woman of chapter 3 is not the woman who is the
basis of the sermon which is found in chapter 2. The
woman of chapter 3 was an adulteress from the beginning
of the story, before she was bought by the prophet. This
is plain and certain, because of the segregation to which
she was committed before there could be any prospect of
cohabitation with the prophet. The idea that the woman
of chapter 3 is Gomer-bath-Diblaim is based on two assumptions for which there is no definite warrant. It is assumed
that Hosea divorced Gomer; this is not stated anywhere,
unless such be the interpretation of 2.2. It is further
assumed that Hosea was buying her back again in chapter
3; this again is not stated, and if it were the case, it would
surely be the most important detail in the whole story.
On the other hand, the picture of Hosea 2.15 envisages the

first pure love of virgin Israel: 'and she shall make answer there (i.e. when she is back once more in the wilderness) as in the days of her youth, and as in the day when she came up out of the land of Egypt.' This is the normal view of the prophets, who regularly take the view that all was well in the old desert days, before Israel entered the land of Canaan and came into contact with the cults of Canaan, Amos 5.25, Jeremiah 2.2, Ezekiel 16.1-34. It may be that chapter 2 is based on the story of chapter 1, assuming that Gomer-bath-Diblaim did not develop her adulterous ways until after the marriage. But this still leaves a cleavage between chapter 3 and chapter 2.

If Gomer-bath-Diblaim is the woman also in chapter 2, then we must assume that she was pure when Hosea married her (cf. 2.15). In this case, we have to deal with 1.2, where Hosea says that he was bidden to marry 'a wife of whoredom and children of whoredom'. Does this necessarily mean that Gomer was a harlot from the beginning and that all her three children were conceived as a result of her harlotry? The verse may be comparable to Isaiah 6.9-12, where Isaiah speaks as if the blindness and deafness to his message was predetermined by God even before the message was delivered. Isaiah is speaking in the light of his experience subsequent to his call. He is confusing, after the manner of more than one Old Testament writer, *post hoc* and *propter hoc*. The net result of his preaching was nil; they did not see, and they did not hear and obey. This happened after (*post*) his preaching, but the prophet writes as though it was because of (*propter*) his preaching. In the same way, it is possible, and indeed probable, that the prophet described Gomer as 'a wife of whoredom' because that was what she turned out to be at a later date, i.e. before the time when he was speaking forth his prophetic messages. Such an explanation would equate the wife of chapter 2 with the wife of chapter 1.

If we assume that Gomer was a harlot when Hosea married her, there is still a difficulty in identifying her with the woman of chapter 3. The natural inference of chapter 1 is that the first child was born within a year or so of the marriage and the others at the usual intervals of two to three years. This could not have happened under the circumstances related in chapter 3.

Another possible solution which has been suggested is that the woman of chapter 3 was bought by the prophet to be a secondary wife, a custom which was legal in Israel according to Deuteronomy 21.15-17. Indeed, according to Leviticus 18.18 (presumably written down and still permissible in the post-exilic period), it was legal for a man to have two wives provided that they were not sisters. Further, the general view of the pantheon worshipped by the Jews of Elephantine in Middle Egypt in the fifth century B.C. is that Jehovah was worshipped there, together with two wives, Anath the chief wife, and (?) Ashimah the secondary wife. This then is a possible solution to the problem, though, if so, it is strange that in the text there is so little evidence for it. It would appear that the only way in which all three chapters can be true to fact is to assume (1) that Gomer was pure at the time of her marriage, but later became an adulteress; (2) that the woman at the basis of chapter 2 is Gomer; (3) that the woman of chapter 3 was intended as a secondary wife. The alternative to (3) is that Hosea divorced Gomer, bought her back from some supposed owner, and placed her in isolation.

All this involves a number of assumptions, so many that it is easier to say that here in these first three chapters we

have three distinct and separate pieces of prophetic teaching which have come to us along three distinct and separate
channels. They are representative of three distinct types of
prophetic teaching, biographical, oracular, and autobiographical. Here we recall Mowinckel's work on Jeremiah.
He held that Type A (oracular and in verse) dated from
the last years of Jeremiah or later (580-450 B.C.), that Type
B (biographical prose) dates from the same period, and
that Type C (autobiographical prose) dates from *c.* 450
B.C., so that it is not only the latest but the least trust-
worthy. The dates will be dates for the completed collections rather than for individual pieces. As we have
indicated above, scholars have questioned Mowinckel's
judgement that Type C was the least reliable, and have
suggested instead that Type B is of least value. It may
well be that Type B is more liable to interpolation (cf.
Hosea 1.7 and again 1.10-2.1), but that on the main issue
Mowinckel after all was right. An unnamed autobio-
graphy can easily be made somebody's biography. In
this way chapter 3 may be much later than the other two
chapters, and not by Hosea at all. It may well be a theme
worked out on the basis of the assumption that Hosea's
wife, Gomer-bath-Diblaim, was originally a harlot ('a wife
of whoredom'), and later worked into the collection of
Hosea's prophecies on the theory that he might well have
used such an illustration and that in any case this is where
a loose piece of prophecy fits best.

Whatever be the truth concerning all these details, the
common theme of the three chapters is plain. Hosea's wife
was found to be a harlot; Israel was found to be similarly
unfaithful to her 'husband'. From his own thoughts concerning his wayward wife, the prophet learned something
of Jehovah's attitude to Israel. He uses the marriage as

an allegory of Jehovah's relation to Israel. The idea of
Israel as the wife of Jehovah is not new with Hosea. His
use of the terms 'my man (*'ishi*)' and 'my lord (master,
ba'ali)' in Hosea 2.16 make it plain that the idea was well
known and well embedded, in point of fact far too well
embedded, in the minds of the people of his day.

The action of the prophet as described in chapter 1 in
naming his children (and also his whole course of action
in chapter 3 if it be held that this chapter is genuinely
from Hosea) is what has been called 'a symbolic action'.
Much has been written concerning these so-called symbolic
actions of the prophets. 'They serve to initiate the
divine activity amid human affairs by performing in minia-
ture that which Yahweh is performing on a larger scale'
(Professor H. W. Robinson, *Inspiration and Revelation in
the Old Testament*, p. 185). Thus the prophet is not to
be regarded as seeking to draw attention to himself and
his message, and then, having gained an audience, to
declare the meaning of it after the manner of an actualized
sermon illustration. Rather the act is regarded as being
in itself effective in bringing God's predetermined deed
into actuality in this material world. It is a development
from the ancient idea of 'Magic'. Early peoples believe
that what is said and what is done is in itself effective in
bringing the desired event to pass. Thus when Isaiah of
Jerusalem (Isaiah 20.2) walked about naked and barefoot
in Jerusalem for three years, he was not only prophesying
the coming captivity of Egypt and Ethiopia, but was
actually ensuring that what God had already in Himself
determined would take place in the realm of human affairs.

But is it true that the prophets actually always acted
out their effective allegories? Did Isaiah really go about
barefoot and either stark naked or in the half-naked garb

of a captive slave for three years, and he a counsellor and companion of kings? He may possibly have done so, though three years is a long time for a man to go about like this. And why three years? And, if he believed his message to have immediate importance, could he, or would he have waited for three years before he declared it? Or again, did Jeremiah (25.17) actually make various nations drink of the cup of the wine of the fury of the Lord? If so, how did he do it? Or yet again, did the author of Zechariah 11.8 really murder three shepherds in one month? In Jeremiah 13 it is stated that Jeremiah made a double return journey to the Euphrates, first to bury a linen girdle there, and then after a considerable time to go and dig it up again. Did he in truth make this long double journey? Possibly, in this case, as some scholars have suggested, the river was Parah, close by Anathoth. This may well have been the case, since there is nothing in the prophet's exposition which involves the idea of exile, and therefore one place would do as well as another for burying the linen. As long as the linen became damp and rotten it did not matter where it was buried, so probably this was a genuine piece of prophetic symbolism. But did Ezekiel actually lie on his left side for forty days and then for another forty days on his right side, cooking during that double period meagre rations on a fire made from dried human excrement? If it be held that this section of that book is not by the Ezekiel who went (or did not go) to Babylonia, then did the author (whoever he was) do all this?

Some of the so-called symbolical actions seem to have taken place in dreams or in the imagination of a prophet so exalted that his state may have verged on a trance. But there is another type of symbolic action, where the prophet

takes an event which has already happened and invests it
with a divine meaning, intention and effectiveness. He
makes it 'a sign and a portent' (Isaiah 8.18), and thus
the age-old combination of myth and ritual is born again
in a combination of Deed and Word which shall be effective
in bringing the divine decision to fruition in the world
of men. This is what Isaiah did in respect of his two sons
when he named them Shear-yashub (a remnant shall repent,
Isaiah 7.3) and Maher-shalal-hash-baz (swift the booty,
speedy the spoil, Isaiah 8.1).

It is probable that Hosea did something of the same
kind of thing with his broken marriage and the three
children. He was married to a wife who, after her marriage
(probably after the birth of her first child), became an
adulteress. Years afterwards, when she had borne in all
three children, Hosea used his own experience as a symbolic
action for the fate of Israel. Israel was unfaithful to
Jehovah just as Gomer was unfaithful to Hosea. Her
children were children of an adulteress just as the Israelites
themselves, land and people, had gone over to the Baal
cults. He gave the three children symbolic names which
form a pattern in exegesis, for all three names seem to have
been chosen at one and the same time. The names are so
framed as to enable the prophet to deliver three progressively serious messages to a wayward people, not so much
threats or warnings as effective words which 'served to
initiate the divine activity amid human affairs'. This is
a much more reasonable assumption than to say that he
gave them their names at birth, and then either uttered
his messages piecemeal or kept quiet for all the years until
the last of the three children had been born.

The name of the first child, Jezreel, stands for the doom
of the royal house of Israel, the dynasty of Jehu, that reck-

less charioteer who drove through blood to the throne. He killed two kings in one day (II Kings 9.24 and 27); he trampled to death Jezebel, daughter and wife of kings (II Kings 9.33); he followed this with the massacre of all Ahab's sons (II Kings 10.14), and he concluded with a general massacre of the worshippers of Baal (II Kings 10. 15-26). But, says Hosea, although he exterminated all the males of the House of Omri, he did not thereby save himself and his house from the penalty of shed-blood. The price of the blood of Ahab's sons must still be paid, just as surely as if Jehu had left alive a male of Ahab's line to be the avenger of blood. Further, the fall of the royal house is taken to involve the fall of the kingdom. This idea that the welfare of the king and the welfare of the state are bound together is found elsewhere in the Old Testament: II Samuel 21.17, cf. I Kings 11.36 and 15.4, etc. The prophet thus pronounced the doom of Israel, interlocking the fate of the royal house and the fate of the kingdom, just as Amos interlocked the doom of the royal house of Damascus with the doom of the Syrian kingdom of which Damascus was the capital (Amos 1.3-5).

This doom is followed by a second portent-name. Scholars have difficulty over the fact that the second child was a girl. There are two possible explanations. The simpler is that the second child of Gomer-bath-Diblaim was actually a girl. The other explanation, if another is desired, is that if the prophet wanted to say something in which Israel was involved as the subject, he was necessarily involved in making it feminine, since although in Hebrew the word 'Israel' is normally masculine, yet Hosea's picture of Israel as the wife of Jehovah involves him in making the word a feminine here. The daughter's name is *Lo-ruhamah*, which is a sentence meaning 'She is not

pitied'. It is a definite denial that God will have any
further tenderness or mercy for Israel. There has, inci-
dentally, been much difficulty over the concluding phrase
of verse 6. Judging by the other two oracles, the explanation of the name Jezreel (verse 4) and the explanation of
the name of the third child (verse 9), the *ki* of the Hebrew
should mean 'because' or 'for' and not 'that', and the
phrase should signify what is going to happen to Israel.
This means that the Revised Version is wrong and that the
Authorized Version is better: 'for I will utterly take them
away' or 'I will carry them clean away'. (This use of the
preposition *lamedh* is unusual, but it is found elsewhere,
Jeremiah 49.29.) If this is the correct translation, then
the reference is to the coming exile, an obvious deduction
for a wise man to make who realized the Assyrian threat
in its full seriousness.

The third child is named *Lo-'ammi*, which is another
short sentence, whereby God categorically denies that Israel
is His people. Hosea therefore speaks of the rejection of
Israel, just as his contemporary Amos did (Amos 9.7). The
three names in chapter 1 therefore tell the story in three
stages of God's rejection of His people Israel, that people
whom God went to redeem to be a people to Him. There
is no hope of any remission of the sentence of doom. The
time for mercy has gone. Israel will cease to be God's
people, and He will cease to be their God. (This involves
the reading of the Revised Version in 1.9. The Hebrew has
'I will not be yours', but the change needed in the Hebrew
is small, and the Revised Version reading is found in two
Greek manuscripts and is supported by Origen and
Augustine.)

Verse 7 is generally regarded as being a later addition
to the genuine words of Hosea. It is the only verse in the

chapter which is plainly rhythmical enough to be reckoned as poetry. It declares that Judah will be saved by the Lord their God, but not by any of the paraphernalia of war. This is the sentiment of Zechariah 4.6 and it springs from utter despair that there will ever be any salvation of Judah by force of arms. The verse is akin to one of the accounts of the unexpected escape of Jerusalem in King Hezekiah's time, when the Assyrian army suddenly disappeared from around Jerusalem, either because of the dreadful slaughter during the night or because Sennacherib was suddenly recalled to Nineveh because of some crisis which had arisen there (II Kings 19.35 and 36). Compare also Isaiah 37.36.

III

THE ESSENCE OF RELIGION

HOSEA may or may not have been the first of the canonical prophets, as the Rabbis supposed, so far as the date of the beginning of his prophetic ministry is concerned. As we have seen, it is possible that Amos began his work as a prophet before Hosea (thus almost all the scholars agree), but there cannot have been any great interval of time between the two beginnings. Hosea and Amos, however, were, as we have seen, certainly the first in time of a new type of prophet in that they spoke and acted always whilst in full possession of their faculties. Men knew them to be prophets in virtue of their words and deeds, not because they went into ecstasies, were subject to fits of ungoverned behaviour, or were at times obviously not in control of themselves.

But there is one respect in which Hosea alone was beyond question the first prophet of a new tradition, and it is this aspect of his work which makes his message of the utmost importance, especially so far as the Bible as a whole is concerned. He realized that religion is first and foremost a matter of relationship with God. The full realization that it is an individual personal relationship with God comes later with Jeremiah. Hosea's contribution is that the relation between God and His people Israel is personal. On God's side it consists primarily of love and compassion and gracious condescension; on man's side, it consists of dutiful love and humble trust. This is to be seen best in a comparison of the teachings of Hosea and Amos, though it is important to realize that in no respect is Hosea antagonistic to Amos. The difference between the messages of the two prophets lies in the realization that when Amos has said all that he has to say, there is still something to be said. This extra something arises out of Hosea's understanding of the personal relationship between God and Israel. At the same time, it is important to realize that it is not 'extra' in the sense of something added on. It is an addition to the teaching of Amos because it was something more about the character and nature of God. It was revealed to Hosea through his own personal experience of a broken-down marriage. Hosea was led to understand this something more about God in a way that Amos was not led. This other 'something' is fundamental.

First, we discuss the similarities between the two prophets. In the first place, Amos and Hosea are at one in realizing that the first move is with God, and that it all began when God brought Israel out of Egypt, or, alternatively, when He found Israel in the wilderness. This is plain in Amos 2.9-10. Here the prophet, speaking in the name of God, is setting forth all that God did for Israel at the beginning of her history. He destroyed the Amorites out of their way, even though they were tall as the cedars and strong as the oaks. The reference here is not to the peoples who were settled east of Jordan, the subjects of Og king of Bashan and Sihon king of Heshbon, as the side-references in editions of the Revised Version suggest. According to Numbers 13.29, the inhabitants of the south were called Amalekites, those who dwelt in the Jordan

Valley and along the coast were called Canaanites, and those who dwelt in the hills were Hittites, Jebusites and Amorites. The tradition of the height and strength of the Amorites is preserved in Numbers 13.28, where they are said to be strong, and where the presence of the giant sons of Anak is mentioned. From the excavations we know that in the third millennium B.C. the Amorites were occupying north Syria, by the Lebanon, and that they spread across east and over the Euphrates. They also spread south into Canaan proper and occupied the area round Shechem (Genesis 48.22). They were responsible as much as any other people for the spread of culture in those early days, and Hammurabi, the best known of all the early Mesopotamian kings, was of Amorite descent. Thus the reference in Amos 2.9 is to the people who inhabited the central highlands at the time of the invasion under Joshua. This was the territory occupied mostly by Ephraim and Manasseh, the two great Joseph tribes, who formed the strength of and were dominant in the northern kingdom of Israel. The wholesale destruction of the original inhabitants of Canaan belongs to the E-tradition and is carried on into the D-tradition.[1] Amos, therefore, is referring to the conquest of the land west of Jordan, and is declaring that, strong and tall though the Amorites traditionally were, the Lord destroyed them root and branch. In 2.10, Amos declares that it was the Lord who brought them up out of Egypt, led them forty years through the wilderness, and finally brought them in to

---

[1] The E-tradition is the Northern tradition. According to the latest opinion, it was oral from c. 750 B.C., and written down at various times till it was finally embodied in the Pentateuch as a whole after the time of Ezra. The D-tradition dates from the time of Manasseh. It consists mostly of the present book of Deuteronomy, the nucleus of which came to light during the restoration of the Temple in 621 B.C.

possess the Promised Land. Further (verses 11 and 12), He raised up the prophets and Nazirites to hold the Israelites faithful to the ways of the God which they had learned in the wilderness.

The same motif is to be found in Amos 3.2, where God is represented as having special knowledge of the children of Israel above all the families of the earth. He brought the whole family of them out of Egypt. There is another reference to the coming out from Egypt in Amos 9.7, but here it is compared with the migration of the Philistines from Crete and of the Syrians from east of Kir. This passage is often taken to mean that the special care which God bestowed on Israel in bringing them out of Egypt is extended to a kindly providence which brought the other two peoples from their original homes. But, as we have argued elsewhere (*Amos* I, p. 37 and II, p. 141), the verse is more likely to signify the rejection of Israel as God's special people. Because of their wickedness and waywardness they are reckoned to Him as being on the same level as Ethiopians, Philistines and Syrians, and the exodus from Egypt as being an ordinary migration and not a special Divine Act.

Hosea also refers to the coming out from Egypt as Israel's earlier association with God (2.15). He also speaks of God as finding Israel in the wilderness: 'I found Israel like grapes in the wilderness; I saw your fathers as the first ripe in the fig-tree at her first season' (9.10): these first-ripe figs that are the sweetest and best of all. There are no tomatoes which taste so good as the first of one's own growing, as many of us well know. There are no figs so good as those first-ripe figs from the fig-tree in its first fruiting season. Similarly the old Israel of the desert was best and dearest of all to God. He found her there

and she was specially His. This wilderness motif without
any reference to the rescue from Egypt, is found in
Deuteronomy 32.10ff. It is also found in Ezekiel and in
some psalms. Possibly it is due to the uniform belief
of the prophets that the pre-Canaan days were Israel's
halcyon time, when all was fair and good, with no terrors
and all was peace. It may be that we have here something of a strand of tradition which did not know an
Egyptian bondage. There are two sources for such a tradition. In the north, there is that element of the northerners
who never left Canaan after Jacob came back from Padan-
Aram, all the Leah tribes except Simeon, Levi and Judah,
and all the concubine tribes, both of Rachel (i.e. Bilhah)
and of Leah (i.e. Zilpah). In the south, there is that mix-
ture of Arab-Edomite clans which, together with Canaanite
elements (Genesis 38.2), formed what was later the tribe
of Judah. This is that southern element, partly Kenite,
in the J-tradition,[1] which Smend identified as J^1, Eissfeldt
as L, Pfeiffer as S, and Morgenstern as K, that element
according to which the sacred Name was known from early
days (Genesis 4.26), and not first at the Bush (Exodus 3.12
in the E-tradition or Exodus 6.3 in the P-tradition). Which
of these two traditions (Egypt or the wilderness only) Hosea
is following is of minor importance in the present connection, because on either basis we have the same insistent
emphasis that God was the Prime Mover in the God-Israel
relation, whether out of Egypt or in the desert. (We
pointed out in an earlier volume, *Hymns of the Temple*,
p. 57, that the first and original datum-line for the God-
Israel relationship was the rescue from Egypt, and that

[1] The J-tradition is the Southern tradition. It goes back to an author
or collector of traditions who flourished in the tenth or ninth century B.C.
Additions were made, chiefly in the pre-exilic period, and it was finally
embodied in the Pentateuch as a whole after the time of Ezra.

the tracing back to Abraham and to Noah of God's election of Israel is a later development.)

The original calling out of Egypt is plain in Hosea 11.1, where the metaphor has ceased to be that of the husband and wife and has become that of father and son. The prophet continues in the third verse with a reference to the guidance through the wilderness in a picture of God the father teaching Israel-Ephraim the son to walk, picking him up in His arms when he tumbled, and soothing the little toddler's bumps and bruises. The reference to Egypt is found once more in Hosea 12.13, where Moses the prophet is God's instrument in bringing the people out of Egypt and preserving them during the subsequent wanderings. This is in the JE-tradition of Deuteronomy 34.10 and also in the northern early post-exilic plea for recognition which is found in Isaiah 63.7-14. (Read the Revised Version margin in verse 11: 'Then his people remembered the ancient days of Moses', and make the small speech end with 'caused them to rest' in verse 14.)

Once again, we get the same statement of God's rescue of Ephraim out of Egypt in Hosea 13.4: 'I am the Lord thy God from the land of Egypt; and thou shalt know (? knowest) no god but me, and beside me there is no saviour,' a sentiment which is reminiscent of many passages in Isaiah 40-55, where the rescue from Babylon is the context with continual reminders of the earlier rescue from Egypt.

Thus we see that Hosea and Amos agree in stating that the first move and the whole initiative was with God. However they may differ in their descriptions of the nature of the relation between God and Israel, they are united in this. We discussed this doctrine of Election in *Hymns of the Temple*, pp. 57-65, together with the implications of the belief in Israelite-Judahite history and religion.

Suffice it to say here that so long as they asked the question: '*When* did God choose us?' all went well, and the farther back they went in order to find the starting-point, the sounder their conclusions were. Further, it was when they began to ask the question: '*Why* did God choose us?' that they began to get into trouble, and the longer they kept on asking that question, the farther they wandered from the truth. If they had remembered the emphasis of Hosea, that it was all due to God's 'loving-kindness' (properly, His *chesed*, see below, pp. 8off.), all would have been well. Indeed, all would have become progressively better and better. But they forgot that they owed everything to God, first, last and all the time in between. They began to think, after the common error of mankind, that it was due to something in themselves. They were prepared to agree that it was 'of grace', but not 'all of grace'. From that point, they began to go wholly and tragically wrong. Mankind, in every genera-tion, goes astray when it forgets, or does not wish to remember, that 'all'.

The second matter upon which Amos and Hosea are in agreement is concerning the penalty for sin. They are both convinced beyond any shadow of doubt, that Israel has nothing to hope for in the immediate future. Exile awaits Israel, and all chance of avoiding this has gone. Whatever message of hope there is in the genuine writings of Hosea, there is no hope of avoiding this national disaster.

Dealing first with Amos, it is agreed by almost all students of his book that Amos 9.11-15 is a later addition and is not at all from Amos, the eighth-century shepherd from Tekoa. The same applies also to such a half-verse as the latter part of Amos 9.8. To continue, Amos throughout is a son of the wilderness with all the desert man's sense of the inexorableness of the desert life. He is strong and ruthless in his condemnations. He could speak in terms similar to those of John the Baptist, of an ' axe that is laid to the root of the trees: every tree therefore that bringeth not forth good fruit is hewn down and cast into the fire ' (Matthew 3.10). Amos speaks similarly of judgement on wrong-doing, and his judgement is swift and immediate, final and complete. For him and for all the prophets, his first message is ' The time is at hand ', and it is followed immediately with that other dreadful word ' Prepare to meet thy God '. Amos's view of the finality of the looming, overhanging judgement is similar to the idea of ruthless destiny to be found in Islam, when, instead of speaking of the Five Pillars of Islam (faith, prayer, alms, fasting, pilgrimage), the essence of Islam is spoken of as being ' Belief in Allah and the Last Day '. There is nothing in Amos to correspond to the parable of Luke 13.6-8, concerning the owner of the fig-tree which bore no fruit. He ordered it to be cut down because it had borne no fruit for three years, but the vine-dresser suggested that the soil round the tree should be well dug and dunged, and that if this treatment brought not fruit, the tree should then be destroyed. Amos would have cut the tree down straightway. So would Hosea, but, as we shall see, where Hosea differed from Amos is that Amos would have burnt the whole tree, whereas Hosea would have cut off a slip and planted it in the hope that a new tree would grow and that possibly the new tree would be more fruitful than the old.

To Amos, God is the stern judge who demands strict moral behaviour and will rigorously punish without any amelioration all lapses from the proper standard of conduct. Amos, therefore, is full of condemnation for offences of man against man. He condemns the surrounding nations one by one for their inhuman and ruthless conduct. Syria-Damascus, Gaza, Ammon, Moab and lastly Israel are in turn condemned. (The oracles against Tyre, Edom and Judah are probably later insertions.) Israel is condemned for selling up the innocent for an odd sixpenny debt or the value of a pair of sandals. Israel is condemned because of the way in which the rich have used the processes of law for the impoverishment of the poor, twisting justice and preventing honest men from giving evidence in the courts. There is prostitution everywhere, either of the temple or of the street. Again and again Amos thunders in judgement against immoral and inhuman practices, mostly on the part of the wealthy ruling classes. The plumb-line is held once more against the wall which originally was built straight and upright with a plumb-line as a guide, and when the wall is found no longer to be true, down it must come (Amos 7.7-9). God will begin at the altar, for that is where the rottenness begins, and He will strike right through the whole land (8.14). No one will escape, wherever he may hide, though they dig down to hell, climb up to heaven, hide in the thick undergrowth of the Ridge of Carmel, sink themselves in the depths of the sea, or even get taken into exile to a land far away. Israel is a basket of *qayits*, the last late ripe summer fruit. This is a sign that the *qeyts*, the full end, is near (8.1-2), because all forbearance has come to an end.

Hosea is equally sure that the sin of Israel is to be punished, though he finds it far from easy to adopt this attitude. It must be realized that Hosea sees that Israel's sin cannot be passed over any more. He speaks in strong terms of condemnation. This needs to be realized and

recognized frankly by all who read the Book of Hosea.
This is what the book says. It is sheer sentiment of the
most dangerous type which suggests that God, because of
His love for Israel, is going to let Israel off from paying the
price of her sin. Such departures from what is written
lead easily to loose sentimental universalist notions which
do not realize that sin is a deadly cancerous growth, for
which there is but one end unless it is taken in hand
ruthlessly and in time.

For Hosea, God's mercy has come to an end. He will
not any longer have compassion on Israel. As we have
pointed out (p. 36), the name *Lo-ruhamah* which Hosea
gave to Gomer's second child is not a statement that Israel
is beyond compassion. It is a deliberate denial that God
will have any compassion upon her. It is not a mere statement that Israel is not 'compassioned', but a deliberate
and strong denial. (The Hebrew is *lo'*, and not *'eyn*.)
In the same way, Hosea 1.9 is a deliberate denial that Israel
is God's people and a definite statement of Israel's rejection by God. In chapter 2 it is stated that the life in
Canaan will come to an end. The corn, the wine, the
wool and the flax will cease. All the harvest feasts will be
finished, since for Israel there will be no harvests, and she
will find herself back in the wilderness once more where
none of these gifts of God are to be found. Or again, in
chapter 4, Hosea's condemnation is as severe as that of
Amos. The penalty of Hosea 4.3 is markedly parallel to
that of Amos 1.2. Amos says there that the Ridge of
Carmel, that most fertile part of the whole country in those
days, the ridge that ran south-east from the promontory by
the sea towards Mount Gilboa, will wither; that is, the last
remnant of greenness will disappear from the whole country.
This is what Hosea says in 4.3: the desiccation will be so

complete that no living thing will be able to continue to
survive. 'The wind hath wrapped her up in its wings
(skirts),' 4.19, and will carry her clear away. God's people
are destroyed because they have not known (4.6), for lack
of that 'knowledge of God' which shows itself in keeping
faith between man and man, and in not murdering and not
thieving and not committing adultery (cf. 4.2). In chapter
5.1-14 also, Hosea is full of threats. Ephraim and Judah
shall both stumble down. God has withdrawn Himself
from them. Though they bring whole flocks and herds for
sacrifices, they will not find Him. God will be like a lion
to Ephraim in that He will carry Ephraim off to destruction
and there is none that will be able to save him. We have
the same attitude in chapter 6.4-11, and again in chapter 7.
The sorry tale of Israel's waywardness is continued in
chapter 8 and again and again in chapters 9 and 10.
Chapter 11.1-7 tells of Israel's persistent apostasy in spite
of all that God had ever done for them. And so it is
throughout the book, for Hosea can see no immediate
future for Israel other than a merited punishment which
is going to mean the end of the nation.

The prophets, one and all, are insistent on this dire
punishment for sin, and they are fully clear that all sin
must be paid for. Nothing else that any of them says
detracts from this. Whatever any of them may say in
addition about the character of God or concerning His ways
with the sons of men, this much is fixed, that He will not
tolerate the kind of behaviour which characterized Israel-
Ephraim during the times of these eighth-century prophets.
Even though we have a prophet like Isaiah of Jerusalem,
who can speak in terms of a 'Remnant shall repent' (Isaiah
7.3), that same prophet can say that the land will be utterly
waste and that the Lord will remove men far away and

that the forsaken places shall be many in the midst of the
land (6.12).

Amos sees no farther than the destruction and exile of
the northern kingdom of Israel. Hosea, too, can see as far
as that, but he can see still farther. He looks forward to
a new beginning, a new Israel. There are scholars (e.g.
Professor Harper in the I.C.C. *Amos and Hosea*) who deny
that any passage which speaks of hope is genuinely from
the prophet Hosea. This is far too sweeping a judgement.
A distinction should be drawn between those passages
which envisage a new beginning for Israel only and those
passages which look for a common revival of Israel and
Judah. Thus we would say that 1.10-2.1 is not from
Hosea ben Beeri. This is not because it is full of hope,
but because it looks forward to a hope of an Israel and a
Judah unified with one common head. This is a southern
expectation. No northerner could possibly look forward
to anything of this kind. The vision of a united kingdom
with a Davidic king belongs to the south. All dreams of
a Davidic Messiah are southern dreams. Similarly, the last
phrases of 3.5 are from a later writer, because they look
forward to a Davidic king. No northerner in his senses
would write or say a thing like that. The oppression of
the north in the time of Solomon would prevent any
thought like that for ever, and even more the actual expression of any such thought. It follows therefore that 3.5,
from at least 'and David their king', is a later and southern
addition. The general opinion is that the rest of the chapter
(3.1-5a 'god') is from Hosea, but, as we have indicated
earlier, we do not think so. We think that the whole of
chapter 3 is late and not from Hosea. The writer thinks,
in this case, that Israel will be well rid of king, (i.e. the
illegitimate king of a non-Davidic line, the kings who

followed in the footsteps of the wicked Jeroboam son of
Nebat), prince, the illegitimate sacrifices offered elsewhere
than at Jerusalem, and those heathen adjuncts to worship
(pillar, ephod, and teraphim) which every good Deuterono-
mist regarded as being worse than useless in their effect on
worship and worshipper. On the other hand, there is no
need at all to doubt the genuineness of 2.15-23 with its
reversal of the condemnations of 1.2-9 and the new turn
given to the names of the children in 1.5, 1.6 and 1.9.
Again, there is no valid reason for rejecting 11.10-11 as a
genuine oracle of eighth-century Hosea. It envisages a
return of Israelites from Assyria and Egypt. Chapter 13.14
is best translated as a series of questions involving the
answer 'No': 'Can I ransom them from the power of
the grave? Can I redeem them from death?' so that
there is no hope at all in this chapter. On the other hand,
there is no need to insist that chapter 14 is from another
and later prophet. It is possible, and indeed likely, that the
last verse is an addition by a devoted, yet puzzled scribe.
How, says he, can these things possibly be true? We
know that these northerners are rebels and apostate from
the true religion of the Jerusalem Temple, and rebels are
bound to stumble in the ways of the Lord; it is the upright
who walk safely in them. Some think that verse 7 (8 in
the Hebrew text) is an insertion, but the text is so uncertain
that it is impossible to say. The verse in the Greek looks
more like a genuine saying of Hosea's: 'they shall return
and dwell under his shadow'. Possibly the conclusion of
the verse originally was 'and they shall flourish like his
well-remembered vine (omitting the article from *kagge-
phen*), like the wine of Lebanon'.

The difference between the two prophets lies in the fact
that whereas Amos thought of God as an all-powerful,

rigorously just lord of the desert, Hosea thought of Him as Husband and Father. For Amos the attitude of God to Israel was typified in the desert which destroys every man who makes a mistake and loses his way. For Hosea, the relation between God and Israel was typified in Hosea's own relation to Gomer-bath-Diblaim. Hosea's experience of married life led him, the first of men, to understand something of the fundamental theme involved in Israel's religion. In Hosea we have the beginning of a line of discovery which reaches down through Jeremiah, some of the psalmists and one phase of Deuteronomic teaching, to reach its full expression and revelation in the life and teaching of our Lord Himself. This conception of religion involves the insistence that behind all demands of morality, and behind all sacrificial customs, there is a personal relationship with God. Morality is important, and sacrificial customs have their place, but a right personal relationship with God is fundamental. This right relationship with God involves, amongst the rest, moral behaviour on the part of man, though here it is far more than is involved in any scheme of equity or give-and-take, and it is not built to any degree upon the rights of the individual. The emphasis is on the motive power behind all demands, ethical or otherwise, the beginning of religion itself, the reason for it and the maintenance of it: all this is to be found in a personal relationship with God. It is true, for instance,[1] that the elements of the teaching of the eighth-century prophets are that Jehovah is Law, Lord of Nature, Lord of History, Lord of the End of Things, Lord of Universal Morality, the God of Israel, the Punisher of Sin and that He makes no ritual demands. All these

[1] Oesterley and Robinson: *Hebrew Religion, its Origin and Development*, 1937 edition, pp. 224-232.

elements are certainly to be found in the writings of these prophets, but the essential element is the special relationship which exists between God and Israel. This, it is true, is mentioned under the heading 'the God of Israel', but it is the most important item in the list. If this were not there, there would be nothing there. Jehovah is Israel's God and Israel's Saviour. He was Israel's Saviour first and all the rest afterwards. This is true historically and it is true essentially in the nature of God. Other religions and the philosophies can say nearly all that is to be found in these prophets concerning Law and Morality, Nature and End in History. But they cannot speak in terms of God as Saviour in the way that Israel's prophets could speak. If we are to understand the preaching of the prophets in general and of Hosea in particular, we must not start from the fact that Jehovah is Law and Morality and the rest. We must start from the fact that He is Saviour. Not only so, but we must start farther back. We must start from the fundamental belief of Israel that Jehovah saved them out of Egypt, brought them through the wilderness, and settled them in the Promised Land, all the time showering upon them the gifts of His bounty and His grace, and all of this for no other reason (as the Deuteronomists saw) than that it was His own goodwill and pleasure. Other religions can speak of a god of law and morality, and many of them do. They can speak of a god who is lord of history and lord of the end of things, and again many of them have done so. A man need be neither Jew nor Christian to know these things about God. The element which is distinctive in these Hebrew prophets is the starting-point, which was in God's love and saving grace, not in His morality. It is true that Jehovah is a God of morality, but we must not say that He is a moral God who loves His

people Israel. Rather, we must say that He is the Lover
of Israel who makes moral (and other) demands upon the
people He loves and has saved. The first emphasis is not
morality, but God's saving work. Morality is a sequel,
not the point of departure.

This primary element and emphasis in Hebrew religion
is visible throughout. The Ten Commandments certainly
embody a moral code, though they are sub-Christian, and
negative rather than positive so far as human relationships
are concerned. They need supplementing for any society
other than the pastoral society for which they were framed.
The first four commandments deal with man's attitude to
God, the fifth with a man's attitude to his parents, and the
remaining five with a man's attitude to his fellowmen.
This is the correct order: God first and then man. No
other god, no images of the One God, no loose use of His
Name, and proper observance of His Sabbath; then
honour your parents, and so to prohibitions that are moral
in the strict sense of the word, actions which have to do
with manners and customs.

But why must Israel obey the Ten Commandments?
The reason given is not because they are morally right,
though this is undoubtedly the case. It is not because such
obedience will be good and beneficial to Israel, though
this is the reason attached to the fifth commandment.
Perhaps it is as well that this reason is not emphasized
in Exodus 20, since human experience shows that adher-
ence to morality does not necessarily bring happiness and
long life in this present world. There are many situations
in which it is certain to bring much sorrow and a speedy
death. The reason is given in the verse which precedes
the Commandments: 'I am the Lord thy God which
brought thee out of the land of Egypt, out of the house

of bondage' (Exodus 20.2). The primary reason, therefore, is that Jehovah was their Saviour from the beginning. This is the reason for Israel's very existence. The essence of the faith, therefore, is not that Israel must act according to the laws of morality because this is a moral universe and God is a God of morality. It is that Jehovah was and is their Saviour, and He has saved them, saves them now in order that they may do His Will. The initial act is God's; it is an act of salvation. Because His initial act is one of salvation, all Israel's acts must conform to the standards involved for men in the character of this Saviour God.

Hosea realized in his own personal life that condemnation and judgement are not the end. It was indeed the end of the first covenant, just as Hosea's marriage with Gomer-bath-Diblaim had come to an end with her faithlessness. Thus he says: 'Plead with your mother, plead; for she is not my wife, neither am I her husband' (2.2). Hosea would not agree with the common homiletical statement that it takes two to break a covenant. It does not take two to break a covenant. It takes two to make a covenant, but only one to break it. Not all the faithfulness of one party can maintain a covenant if the other party does not adhere to the terms of the arrangement. Hosea's covenant with Gomer came to an end with her persistent adultery. In the same way God's covenant with Israel came to an end with Israel's persistent apostasy. But Hosea was prepared to make a fresh start; he was prepared to enter into a new covenant. Thus Hosea knew that God also was prepared to begin again with Israel and to enter into another covenant with her. He knew this because of his own love for his erring wife; not all her adulteries could destroy his love for her. The same is true of God and Israel. It is another case of 'if ye then, being evil, know how to give good gifts unto your children, *how much more* shall your Father which is in heaven give good things to them that ask him?' (Matthew 7.11).

If only, thinks Hosea, he and Gomer could go back again to those first days, then perhaps all would be well. He remembers, to use the expression of Jeremiah 2.2, 'the love of their espousals'. Similarly, God remembers Israel's first marriage love, and how faithfully, loyally, and dutifully she followed God in the wilderness. Hosea is certain that Israel will lose the land which God once gave to her, the land of Canaan with its corn and wine and oil, all the fruits of fertility which the wilderness never knew. Israel will find herself east of Jordan once more. God will entice her and bring her back again into the wilderness. There, once more, He will make love to her (2.14). And (verses 6 and 7 should probably be transferred hither) he will hedge up her way so that she cannot get back to her lovers in Canaan; till at last she will say that after all she was better off at first before she ever knew anything about the Baals of Canaan, when she knew only her true husband, Jehovah. Then she will find out her big mistake. All along, ever since she was first given the corn and the wine and the oil of Canaan, she thought that these were the gifts of the Baals. That was why she lavished these gifts on the Baals. She followed the ways of the inhabitants of Canaan, and she did what they did. She never knew that it was Jehovah who had given her all these things. When she has turned to Jehovah again, He will give her all these things. He will give her vineyards once more (2.15) from the wilderness. The Valley of Achor (trouble) by which she entered Canaan for the first time (Joshua 7.24 and 26) will be an entrance for her a second time, but this second time it will be a Door of Hope—hope for a future characterized with a new trust and a true loyalty, wherein a people of a new faithfulness will be truly thankful to a Husband-God who has never been anything else than faithful from the beginning.

The rendering of the old Greek Version (Septuagint) is somewhat different from the Hebrew in 2.15. These differences need to be noticed in Hosea, because the Hebrew text of Hosea is more disturbed and corrupt than the text of any other part of the Old Testament. The result of this is that many sections are very disjointed in the Hebrew, and some verses are unintelligible. Fortunately, in some cases where the Hebrew means nothing, the Greek gives a very satisfactory meaning, and it is probable that in these instances the text of the Greek Version is much closer to the original. Here in 2.15, the Greek says that God will give her the Valley of Achor to open her understanding, 'and she shall be afflicted there according to the days of her infancy'. The message as a whole is still a message of hope, though the Greek translators (? interpreters) thought of the renewed sojourn in the wilderness as a time of punishment and trial for the most part. It is probable that the Hebrew here is sounder than the Greek. As we have seen, to the prophets generally, the earlier sojourn in the wilderness was Israel's halcyon day. The Greek interpretation here is influenced by thoughts of other days and other lands, and is the work of men who take the normal view of people in a settled country that the desert is all that is hard and undesirable.

When Israel comes back into Canaan once more, some at least of the old temptations will be removed. The name of Baal will be cut wholly out of the vocabulary. Israel will no longer refer to God as *Ba'ali* (my lord), but as *'Ishi* (my man). This new covenant will bring complete happiness and prosperity. There will be a league of fruitfulness with all living creatures and no wars to bring trouble and misery. The earth will respond with corn and wine and oil. The name Jezreel will have its proper meaning. It will stand no more for the dire retribution which by that time will have overtaken the House of Jehu (1.4), but it will mean what it says, 'El shall sow.' Israel shall be sown in the land to be God's own harvest. Formerly, the prophet had to deny that Israel would receive any mercy and compassion. Now Hosea must deliberately deny his previous denial. God will have compassion upon her (2.23). And similarly, this new Israel is clearly declared to be God's people (cf. 1.9) and Israel will confess that Jehovah is her God.

Thus we see that Hosea equals Amos in his stern condemnation of sin, and equals Amos also in his certainty of full and unavoidable punishment for it, but he goes on from that to a hope for a new beginning, a new covenant when all shall be well between God and His people, and Israel shall know the happiness and the peace which is proper to the People of God in the Land of Promise.

Hosea's hope for a better future after the time of punishment assumes another form in 5.15. This verse is preceded by a passage where God is represented as being fully active in Israel's destruction: God will be like a ravening lion whom none can rob of its prey. Verse 15 continues: 'I will go and return to my place, till they have paid the price and then seek my face.' Here God is not represented as being active in Himself procuring a new attitude on the part of Israel or in doing anything to bring Israel back to Him. Perhaps this is partly because the prophet cannot be saying everything all the time, but the natural meaning of this particular piece is that the prophet expects that the

punishment itself will be sufficient. Perhaps the idea is
that when the penalty involved in the sin is paid, then the
slate is clean and a new start can be made. This is very
likely, since the Hebrew word which is used, translated
above as 'they have paid the price' ('acknowledge their
offence' in the Revised Version, with 'have borne their
guilt' in the margin), is the root *'asham*. The noun from
this root is used in the post-exilic period as a technical term
for one of the 'sin-offerings' of the Levitical system. The
word *'asham*, usually translated 'guilt-offering', is used
in connection with offences where the damage can be estimated in cash or kind. The ordinary *'asham* (guilt-offering)
was a ram, together with restitution plus one-fifth of the
value of the object involved. This particular form of offering seems to have been unknown in the pre-exilic period,
but the root is known, both as noun and verb. It occurs
in the passage where we find the account of the return of
the Ark to Israel by the Philistines with an *'asham* of
golden rats and boils, images of those inconveniences which
had plagued the Philistines ever since they had captured
the Ark (I Samuel 6.3, 4, 8, 17). The same idea of payment in cash by way of compensation is found in II Kings
12.17. In Isaiah 53.10 the word *'asham* is used of the
sufferings of the Servant of the Lord. Here, as in the cases
previously cited, there is no connection whatever with the
guilt-offering of the Priestly Code and the Second Temple.
The passage means, 'When you realize that he (the
Servant) has suffered for you (cf. verses 5 and 6), then he
will be assured of a posterity for a long time and the Will
of God will come to fruition through him.' There is no
reference here to any temple ritual, just as neither the lamb
led to the slaughter nor the sheep to the shearer has a temple
reference. Similarly here in Hosea 5.15, the reference is

to Israel paying the full penalty for her sin, paying the price and obtaining quittance from the sin when the full penalty has been paid. Not yet have we come to the theme of Isaiah 53 with its vicarious payment of the penalty. Israel had much to learn before any prophet was in a position to receive such knowledge as that. Hosea's understanding of the relation between sin and suffering is that man must pay the price. It still is true that the price has to be paid.

The Hebrews, at least the prophets and the authors of Scripture generally, were very clear about the connection of sin and suffering. How much earlier there were Hebrews conscious of this, earlier, that is, than the time when the various parts of the Bible were written, it is impossible to say. But the idea is certainly embedded in the language. For instance, Cain says, 'My punishment is greater than I can bear' (Genesis 4.13). The word used for 'punishment' is *awon*, a word which is usually translated 'iniquity'. There are many other cases of this use of the word: e.g. Isaiah 5.18, I Samuel 28.16, Isaiah 40.2 and many other instances. There is a similar use of the word *chet'*, normally translated 'sin'; e.g. Isaiah 53.12, Lamentations 3.39, etc. Even the word *pesha'*, normally, though wrongly, translated 'transgression' (the true meaning is 'rebellion') is used in the sense of the consequences of sin in Daniel 8.12, 13, and 9.24. The idea of sin bringing its own punishment in its train, a penalty which must of necessity be paid, is ingrained in the Hebrew mind, but the insistence upon it and the development of the idea of the connection is due to the prophets, beginning with these men of the eighth century, Hosea and Amos. When the penalty has been paid, the sinner is clear and all is well. God has laid down that all sin in this world must be paid for, and, as Miss Dorothy Sayers once phrased it, 'God was man enough to take His own medicine.'

The hope of a new beginning and better times is shown at its brightest, so far as Hosea is concerned, in 6.1-3. Possibly these three verses are a continuation of 5.15, though it seems to be a separate piece, happily inserted here, but nevertheless a genuine oracle of the eighth-century Hosea. The small section fits in most admirably as the confession of those who are convicted and converted by their suffering (cf. 5.15). The Revised Version margin suggests that the word 'saying' should be inserted in order to make sure that these verses are understood to have been spoken by the repentant Israelites of 5.13. (This habit of inserting 'saying' is dangerous and can be wholly misleading. It has been inserted wrongly, for instance, in Psalm 2.2-3, where it is not the heathen rulers who say verse 3, since they were never in bondage to Israel. It is Israel who speaks verse 3, because Israel is going to break the bonds of the heathen when King Messiah is established on the holy hill of Zion. Similarly, it is a mistake to introduce the word 'saying' before Isaiah 53.1. This fifty-third chapter is not what the heathen kings say; it is what Israel says, realizing that the Servant has suffered for the sins of Israel-Judah in the days of the kingdoms.)

Chapter 6.1-3 goes farther than 5.15. In 5.15 God says that He will return to His place to wait until the people turn and seek Him. The reference is not to His place in Jerusalem, since this is a northern prophet who would have no use for Jerusalem. It is not to His place in heaven, but to the Mountain of the North, the fabled Mount of God, where He lives in His mighty palace, earthly models of which He permits to be built on the high hills of Canaan so that men, by proxy so to speak, can come to worship Him there. Deuteronomy later said that Zion alone on earth is His holy hill. In 6.2 we have God active in bringing the dead or dying Israel to new life. Perhaps the two go together, and 5.15 intends to say that Israel must first turn, and then God will be active in her restoration. Possibly this repentance is involved in 6.2, but in any case it is plain that the Lord will be very active in Israel's new resurrection life. After a short while, God will make her come to life again; He will give her new life. Israel is to know and to grow in knowledge of the Lord, and He will come to Israel like the seasonal rains, those spring rains which stir the whole land into new growth and fertility.

The use of the root *yada'* (know) is important here. We are accustomed to follow the Greek tradition and to interpret knowledge as being mainly intellectual. The Hebrews did not do this. With them knowledge was personal rather than intellectual. This is to be seen in the use of the word to mean sexual intercourse, e.g. Genesis 4.1 and frequently both of the intimacies of married life and of irregular associations. The use of the root *yada'* is naturally wide, and it includes all types of knowledge, though the intellectual aspect is largely catered for by the root *bin*. Hosea here envisages a growingly intimate personal knowledge of God. Amos used the same word in Amos 3.2, a verse which is important, not only because it is an early declaration of God's special and peculiar interest in Israel, but also because it is the one verse where there may be said to be any indication of intimacy in Amos's descriptions of the relation between God and Israel. Amos is apparently intending to say something about a special knowledge which God has of Israel, a knowledge which implies a certain amount of intimacy, but it is uncertain how much of this can fairly be read into his use of the word here. Elsewhere, as we have seen, Amos thinks of Jehovah as the inexorable Judge without any measure of kindliness or 'bowels of mercy'.

We are left with two passages which speak of restoration, certainly chapter 14 and possibly chapter 11.1-11. Chapter 14 is a general call to repentance where Israel is bidden to turn back again to God in penitence. Her prayer is to be (14.2): 'Take away altogether (our) iniquity' (the Hebrew is difficult here, and the Septuagint may preserve the original: 'Thou canst take away iniquity'); 'and accept what is good' (once more the Hebrew is difficult: possibly we should read 'that we may receive good'), 'and we will pay in full the fruit of our lips' (i.e. fulfil the vows we make. Hebrew has 'bullocks' as against the Greek 'fruit of'). 'Assyria cannot save us, and we will not trust in chariots' (lit. 'drive, or ride, on a chariot-horse'; the reference is to the armed support continually being offered by Egypt); 'no more will we say to our own handiwork "our Gods", for it is in thee that the fatherless find compassion' (the last phrase may be a later addition). God then promises healing and the utmost generosity of His love. The section ends (verses 5 and 6) with a promise of all the fertility that Palestine can offer.

The other passage (11.1-11) may or may not be hopeful, but it is of great value in that it shows why it is that God is prepared to begin again with Israel. The prophet changes over from the metaphor of husband and wife to that of father and son. Unfortunately the Hebrew text is often difficult and is sometimes untranslatable. It is a great pity that in the Hebrew text the passage is so badly preserved. Fortunately, in the case of some of the difficult lines the Greek text helps considerably, but even then there are some lines that remain wholly uncertain. Some scholars say that there is no hope at all in the chapter. Others are of the opinion that the message of hope is prominent. The chapter reads:

When Israel was a child, then I came to love him, and I called him from Egypt to be my son. As often as I called them, they turned away from me (so the Greek). They sacrificed to the Baalim, and burned their offerings in smoke to the idols. Yet it was I who taught Ephraim to walk, and (when they tumbled) I took them on my arms (so the Greek) and they did not know that I healed them. With cords of man (? truth) I drew them, with ropes of love, and I was to them as one who takes off the yoke from their jaws and puts food before them (this is probably the sense, though it involves various changes in the Hebrew. The Greek is not helpful: 'I will be to them as a man smiting on his cheek, and I will look to him, I will prevail with him', unless the reference is to the driver of a young beast, using a stick when the animal will not respond to the guiding of the reins.) He shall not return to the land of Egypt (the Greek has 'Ephraim dwelt in Egypt'). Assyria must be his king, for they have refused to return to me. A sword shall whirl in his cities, and shall destroy his bars (i.e. the bars of the city gates), and shall devour in their fortresses. (The whole verse is uncertain. The Greek is no help, but the general sense appears to involve threats of certain disaster and widespread destruction.) My people are hung up to turning away from me. (Perhaps this is what the Hebrew means, but the difficulty of the Hebrew may be judged from the rendering of the Greek: 'and his people are hanging over their dwelling'.)

(The rest of verse 7 is unintelligible.)   How can I let thee
go, O Ephraim?   How can I surrender thee, O Israel?
How can I treat thee as Admah, or make you like
Zeboim?   (The Greek says that God will make them
like these two cities of the Plain which tradition says
suffered the same fate as Sodom and Gomorrah.)   I will
not act according to the fury of my wrath: I will not
return to destroy Ephraim.   (Some scholars see here two
questions, thus turning these two statements into threats
of destruction.   To complicate the matter still further it is
possible to take 'how' throughout to be an exclamation
and not an interrogative.   This has the effect of turning
the verse into a statement of coming destruction by God,
instead of making it expressive of God's dilemma.)   For
I am God and not man, the Holy One in your midst
and not mortal.   (? The reference in the Hebrew to the
city is difficult, though here the Hebrew and the Greek
agree.   The translation offered follows the suggestion
of Volz, and is supported by Nowack and Harper.)
(Verses 10 and 11 are strange, since verse 11 gives a
promise of restoration, saying that they will come out
of Egypt, whereas in verse 5 it is denied that they will
go to Egypt.   Further, the idea of the lion roaring as
a call to come is most unusual and strange, and it is
stranger still that the people should come from the west.
There seems to be no alternative to giving up the verses
as hopeless.   They appear to be a series of confused
additions.)

Nevertheless, confused and uncertain as so much of
chapter 11 is, we do find in it more clearly than anywhere
else in the book an explanation of Hosea's thoughts concerning Israel's future.   He is sure of Israel's destruction

C

and at the same time he is fervently hoping and expecting a revival and resurrection of the people. The confusion among the translators is a true reflection of the dilemma in which Hosea finds himself. His demand for right conduct and his knowledge that the covenant is broken by Israel's wrong conduct conflict throughout with his knowledge that the true lover can never cease to love his loved one. His own love for Gomer was as strong at the end as it was at the beginning. Hosea knows that God's love for Israel is no less strong, and his hope is that it can be more effective. He is sure that Israel's waywardness and apostasy can never cause God's love for her to cease.

All this arises out of Hosea's knowledge that the key to the problem of God's dealings with Israel is to be found primarily in His love for Israel, and only secondarily in His ethical demands. If there was no more to be said than that God demands right conduct, there would be no slightest hope for Israel. For them, and also for us, the story of divine redemption would have ceased almost before it was begun. It is because the essential characteristic of God, overriding all others in importance, is that He is love, that there is hope for the redemption of the sinful nation. This applies to all individuals in all time, equally as to all nations in all time.

In Mark 12.28-34 we have the story of a scribe who came to our Lord Jesus and asked Him, 'What commandment is the first of all?' The reply is curious and significant. Jesus did not turn to Exodus 20 and pick out one of the Ten Commandments. He did not go to the parallel passage in His favourite Deuteronomy (cf. 5.6-21). He quoted from Deuteronomy 6.4-5: 'Hear, O Israel; the LORD thy God, the LORD is one: and thou shalt love the LORD thy God with all thy heart and with all thy self and

with all thy strength.' Jesus then added another passage of
Scripture which He said was the second greatest commandment. Once more He quoted neither from Exodus 20 nor
from Deuteronomy 5. He quoted part of Leviticus 19.18:
'Thou shalt love thy neighbour as thyself.' And He concluded His answer by saying: 'There is none other commandment greater than these.' When they talked about
doing or not doing, Jesus talked about loving God in the
first place, and about loving one's neighbour in the second
place. The reason for this is not that Jesus had no interest
in what men did or said, but that He knew the main-
spring of all action to be a firm love for God.

This is true to human experience. A husband, for
instance, may be unfaithful to his wife. Why? There
is no need to study great volumes on ethics in order to
know the answer, nor is there any need to consult a
psychiatrist. The answer is very simple and plain. He
loves that sort of thing better than he loves his wife. If
he loved his wife, he would be faithful to her. Until
he loves his wife better than he loves that sort of thing,
there is little likelihood of his ever changing his ways. No
punishment and no penalty can change him. Moral
exhortations are useless. But as soon as he comes once
more to love his wife, there will be no need to talk to him
about the necessity of reform. He will already have
reformed his conduct.

Or again, in I John 5.3 there is a statement to the effect
that 'His commandments are not grievous'. This all
depends upon whether we want to do them or not.
Further, our wanting to do them depends upon whether
we love God. If we truly love God, then no commandments of His are grievous. If we do not love God, then
any commandment of His, whatever it is and however

slight, is liable to become a burden too heavy to be borne. It is not always enough to command a man to do what is right. It is not always enough to convince him by argument that such and such a course of action is right. In the last resort there must be an emotional content for action. This is why reasoned statements so often break down. Here it is that all barely ethical systems break down. There is always the gap between 'ought to do' and 'do'.

The secret of any reformation either in the individual or in a group large or small is in the emotions. Men must become enthusiastic; their emotions must be stirred. They must be whipped up by hatred or transformed by love. This is because they are living beings, persons and not automata. And God is a Person, not an abstraction. To say that God is Truth, Beauty and Goodness is doubtless a sound statement, but Truth, Beauty and Goodness, ideal and splendid though they be, are not enough to make men adhere to any one or all three. To talk in terms of Values does not bring men to the point of action. In any case, the essence of Christianity is to be found in the Cross, in the story of a God who so loved the world that He gave His only begotten Son. It is a matter of God loving every man with an everlasting love, of His seeking to save that which is lost, of His dying upon the Cross for every son of man.

To the Jews this a stumbling-block and to the Greeks it is foolishness. It still is foolishness to all who walk in the footsteps of the Greeks, to all who talk in terms of Truth, Beauty and Goodness as the 'three values', and who desire that all things should be balanced, aesthetically harmonious and ethically good. There is no beauty in the Cross. It is a nasty, ugly, cruel, ghastly mess. There is no elegance there, but stark tragedy. The man who wishes to find God can look at a beautiful countryside in the autumn with its russets and gold; he can look at the stars above and all the beauties of earth and sea, but he still will be as far away as ever from knowing the God and Father of our Lord Jesus Christ. If any man would see God, he must look to the Cross. There he will see what really matters about God. He can see there that behind all talk of good conduct and brotherly love, excellent as these things are, there is a God who dies for men because He loves them. And to love God with all that a man is and has, is more than all burnt offerings and sacrifices, more indeed than anything else.

IV

THE SECOND MARRIAGE

IF, AND WHEN, the marriage relationship between
Jehovah and Israel is restored, what guarantee is there that
Israel will be any different from what she was before?
According to Hosea 2.15 God will give Israel 'vineyards
from thence' in such a way that it will be plain to Israel
that she owes them to Jehovah and not to the Baalim. But
what guarantee is there that when Israel comes once more
into Canaan, she will not be enticed away by the cults of
Canaan and her whole environment, so that her last state
will be no whit better than her first?

Hosea realizes that God will have to do something more
than was done before. He says (2.19): 'And I will betroth
thee unto me for ever; yea, I will betroth thee unto me
with' (the Hebrew preposition *beth* here means not 'in',
but 'with the price of': it is *beth pretii*) 'a bridal price
of *tsedeq*' (translated 'righteousness' in the Revised Version), '*mishpat*' ('judgement'), '*chesed*' ('loving-kindness') 'and *rachamim*' ('mercies'). If Israel had possessed
these originally, there would never have been any break-
down of the first covenant, nor any necessity for her to be
exiled from the land which Jehovah had given her. These
four qualities are the conditions under which the new marriage covenant can be established and maintained.

What then is the meaning of these four Hebrew words?

70

First *tsedeq* (or its feminine form *tsedaqah*). We have discussed this word elsewhere at length.[1] The usual translation in our English Bibles is 'righteousness', though occasionally 'justice' is found. These renderings are for the most part inadequate, and sometimes wholly misleading. There are instances, especially in Isaiah 40-66, where the parallelism of Hebrew verse shows that the word means 'victory, salvation', e.g. Isaiah 41.2, 10, 45.8, 62.1, etc.; also Psalm 40.10, 132.9, together with some forty or fifty other cases. The important factor in the understanding of the word is that it signifies that which conforms to the norm. Thus a stone (i.e. a weight) that is *shelemah* (complete, full) and *tsedeq* is one which conforms to the standard weight (Deuteronomy 25.15). It is not *tsedeq* because it conforms to a moral and ethical standard (though ethics are of course involved), but because it conforms to the standard of what the particular weight should be. Similarly, in the same verse, an ephah which is *shelemah* and *tsedeq* is an ephah-measure (a little more than a bushel) which conforms to the standard of what an ephah should be. Or again, 'sacrifices of *tsedeq*' (Deuteronomy 33.19, Psalms 4.5 and 51.19) are not sacrifices offered by worshippers whose conduct is morally sound (though it is hoped that this is the case), but sacrifices in the offering of which all the detailed regulations have been fulfilled. They are 'correct' sacrifices, both valid and regular. An outstanding example of the use of the root is to be found in Genesis 38.26, where Judah declares that Tamar has been more 'righteous' than he. From a strictly ethical point of view, there was not a very great deal to choose between

[1] See the article 'Righteousness' in *A Theological Word Book of the Bible* (S.C.M. Press, 1950), pp. 202-4. For a fuller treatment, see *The Distinctive Ideas of the Old Testament, Norman Snaith* (Epworth Press, 5th edition, 1953), pp. 51-78.

them, and the conduct of both of them left a great deal to be desired. Neither of them could really be considered 'righteous' in any ethical sense that is worth anything. Tamar had dressed up as a prostitute, waylaid Judah and was with child by him. Tamar was more 'righteous' than Judah, because she had conformed more closely to the standards of conduct of the period; at least she had shown to Judah that his conduct had fallen gravely short of the proper standard. Judah should, by that time, have married Tamar to his third son. Her justification for her conduct was that she had acted as she had done in order to point out to him the injustice which he had done her in leaving her a widow for so long.

The meaning of *tsedeq-tsedaqah* therefore depends upon the norm that is taken. It means right behaviour, but the word 'right' has to be defined. It is here that the religion of the Bible (i.e. the prophets of the Old Testament and the New Testament as a whole) differs from so much that generally passes for religion even within Christendom. The meaning of the word is usually taken to be 'righteousness' in the sense of what is plainly ethical and of the standard of the best human conduct. The effect of this is to be seen in the note on *dikaiosune* (the usual New Testament translation of the word is 'righteousness') in Sanday and Headlam's *Romans* (*International Critical Commentary*, pp. 28-31). It is there stated that the limited Platonic use and meaning of the word 'had a long and decisive influence on the whole subsequent history of the word in the usage of Greek philosophy, and of all those moral systems which had their roots in that fertile soil'. They say also that this tendency was further intensified in Roman tradition, because the Latin tongue has no equivalent for the wider meaning of *dikaiosune*. It therefore fell

back on *justitia*.　Further, although Christian thought was
of course influenced by what it found in the Bible, yet it
quoting Sanday and Headlam again) 'could never wholly
throw off the limiting conditions of its origin'.　That is,
Christian ideas of 'righteousness' have not been wholly
free from the influence of the Latin *justitia* and the narrower
usage of Plato.　Our contention is that orthodox Christian
thought has never truly broken free from the shackles of
the classical tradition, not only in its understanding of
the word *dikaiosune* and its Hebrew counterpart *tsedeq-
tsedaqah*, but also in its general approach to the understanding of religion.　The custom is still to do what
Western Christendom has done, namely, to start with half
of its list of virtues derived 'through Cicero from the Stoics
and Plato'.　The result is that for many devout Christians
it tends to be essentially a human virtue—that which all
men of goodwill hold to be acceptable—since, even if we
allow for it the wider Greek significance of Aristotle and
equate 'righteousness' with the 'highest virtue' (*teleia
areta*), it still is defined as *pros heteron* (duty *towards one's
neighbour*) (cf. Aristotle, *Nichomachean Ethics* V. i. 15).
Nobody in his senses would deny that this is a splendid
ideal, but it is a human ideal.　Whilst it is the product
of the greatest minds of Greece, reinforced by the greatest
minds of the classical tradition, it still is a product of human
thought and an idealization of all that is considered best in
human conduct.　But splendid as all this is, it has never
lost the limitations of the Latin *justitia*, with the result that
generosity is thought of as a virtue above the average,
reflecting extra credit upon the generous man, but by no
means necessary if a man would pass the regular ethical
tests.　Generosity tends to be a work of supererogation, and
therefore deserving more than ordinary commendation.

Such a man is often claimed to be a saint as distinct from an ordinary Christian, since the tendency is to identify right conduct with Christian conduct. Thus it comes about that there is little noticeable difference between the normal conduct of a good Jew, a good Muslim and a good Christian. The standard is the general Stoic standard. But in the prophets and subsequently in all the rest of the Bible which has been influenced by the prophets, the norm is not a standard of human conduct. The norm is God Himself. If therefore we are to understand the biblical meaning of *tsedeq*, we must first study the Nature of God Himself.

Here we must turn to these eighth-century prophets in the first instance, and point out that already the meaning of *tsedeq* is at least as wide as the meaning of *dikaiosune* in Aristotle, and much wider than in Plato and the Stoics. In fact, already the word has more of generosity in it than the *dikaiosune* of Aristotle. It is necessary also to realize that in Hebrew religion the development was always wider and wider, instead of narrower and narrower as it was in Greek philosophical thought (cf. the quotations above from Sanday and Headlam's *Romans*). The word in the eighth-century prophets ' shows a persistent tendency to topple over into benevolence, and easily to have a special reference to those who stand in dire need of a Helper'.[1] This emphasis can be seen in such passages as Isaiah 11.4: 'With righteousness shall he judge the poor, and reprove with equity for the meek of the land.' In Amos 2.6 the specific charges of the prophet are of selling up the poor in foreclosure of the smallest of debts. Everywhere the prophets are condemning the exploitation by the rich of the poor, either by open rapacity or by ' seeded' justice. It is of

[1] *The Distinctive Ideas of the Old Testament*, p. 77.

course true that if right-dealing and equity are to be established in the land, most attention must necessarily be given
to those elements in the public life where there is least
right-dealing and equity. Whatever the reason for it,
the fact nevertheless is that from the time of the eighth-
century prophets, the words *tsedeq-tsedaqah* inclined more
to the idea of ' salvation' rather than that of ' strict justice'.
Thus in Psalm 103.6, we read: ' The Lord executeth
righteous acts and judgements for all that are oppressed.'
See also Psalm 146.5-10, where the whole emphasis is on
God's 'judgement for the oppressed' and His care for the
resident alien ('stranger'), the fatherless and the widow.
As a result of this, in New Testament times the word
tsedaqah means ' benevolence', ' almsgiving', and it can
actually be contrasted with ' justice'. This can be seen
in Daniel 4.27, where *tsidqah*, the Aramaic equivalent,
equals ' shewing mercy to the poor'. Compare also the
Authorized and the Revised Versions at Matthew 6.1 and
the passage in the Jewish *Tosephta Sanhedrin* i, 3:
' Wherever there is justice (*din*), there is no *tsedaqah*, and
wherever there is *tsedaqah*, there is no *din*.'

An instructive instance of the use of the word *tsedaqah*
is to be found in Deuteronomy 24.13. The passage is concerned with loans and pledges, especially in the case of a
borrower who is poor. The only piece of property he can
give as a pledge is his cloak, in which he wraps himself
during the day and sleeps in at night. The law says that
the lender must return the borrower his cloak at dusk, so
that the borrower will have some protection against the
cold of the night. And this, says verse 13, is *tsedaqah*
('righteousness'). Certainly, it is not justice, because the
lender had every right to the cloak till the loan was repaid.
Tsedaqah here already is a kindliness which far outstrips

strict justice. Deuteronomy 24.13, in fact, is the parent of the passage from the *Tosephta Sanhedrin*, quoted in the last paragraph. That passage is certainly in the true Old Testament tradition of 'righteousness'.

The upshot of all this is that inherent in *tsedaqah* there is from the eighth-century prophets onwards a warmth and a depth that is absent from the regular philosophical usage which is the seed-bed of the classical tradition. The word has a religious content rather than an ethical content. By this, we mean that its meaning has to be found in the nature of God rather than in customs and speculations of man, however noble and splendid these thoughts and ideals may be at their best. Thus the man who acts morally so far as his own actions are concerned, and acts with fairness and equity towards his neighbour, is not necessarily a Christian. He may be a Jew, a Muslim, a Parsee, a Confucianist, anything or nothing religiously. The Christian is the man for whom such excellent conduct is below the standard, because the God of the Christian is not primarily a moral God. He is a moral God, but to say this is to speak about only the outskirts of His Presence. First and foremost He is the Saviour God, the Lifter-up of the fallen, the Upholder of the fatherless and the widow, the One whose first and greatest deed for Israel was to rescue him from the 'house of bondage', whose attitude to Israel is characterized by more than justice and right-conduct, whose attitude is characterized by that steadfast determination, so evident in Hosea's writings, to begin again from the beginning that He may perchance save Israel even from herself.

In the same way, the word *mishpat* ('judgement') is to be interpreted by reference to God and not by reference to any human considerations of equity and justice between

man and man, so that every man 'gets his rights' and so
forth. As we have pointed out,[1] *mishpat* properly is
judgement by precedent. The nearest to it in English
is case law. The verdict in a British court at all levels is
given in accordance with precedent. It is well known that
in cases of more than ordinary complexity the judge at
Assizes or in the High Courts will 'reserve his judgement'.
This is so that he may take every precaution and consult
all available authorities in order that the judgement he
finally delivers is, so far as may be, in accordance with what
has been said before, that is, truly in accordance with precedent. For us in our British civil courts, it is the Queen's
Justice that is maintained. The important factor in the
Hebrew meaning of *mishpat* is that fundamentally all
justice is God's Justice. The Queen's Justice is no Consti-
tution that can be found in this or that document plus
these or those amendments. It is composed of all the
decisions which have been given as far back as memory
and records go, implemented or perhaps on occasion transformed by such Acts of Parliament as may have been
thought necessary for the public well-being. The norm is
human experience as it has worked out from generation
to generation. This, of course, is partly true of ancient
Hebrew law, but in the hands of prophets *mishpat* has its
basis in the Nature and Character of God. There was
always this God-centred motif amongst the Hebrews.

There is, for instance, the tradition to be found in the
later strand in the Books of Samuel, where Samuel is
against the idea of a king being appointed: 'Ye said unto
me, Nay but a king shall reign over us: when the Lord
your God was your king' (I Samuel 12.12). In the earlier

[1] Cf. the article on 'Judge, Judgement' in *A Theological Word Book
of the Bible*.

strand the word *nagid* is used, translated 'captain' in the Authorized Version and 'prince' (margin 'leader') in the Revised Version (cf. I Samuel 9.16, etc.). In Ezekiel 40-48, that 'blue-print' of the Zadokites for the new order, the word *nasi'* ('prince') is used (e.g. Ezekiel 46.2, etc.), all the time in order to avoid the use of the word 'king' of any earth-born man. When Hilkiah the priest produced a scroll of the law in the reign of King Josiah, the king sent Hilkiah and the court officials to consult Huldah the prophetess (II Kings 22.14-20). Her reply (verse 15) began 'Tell ye the man that sent you unto me . . .', when she knew very well that 'the man' was the king. There was thus always a strong theocratic element in Hebrew thinking, so that the idea of God's Justice was always strong.

Thus it is the word *mishpat* (judgement by precedent) tends to have this God-given basis. This is how the word can be used of the 'ordinance' of the migratory birds. The stork, the turtle dove, the swallow and the crane all observe 'the time of their coming'. This is their *mishpat*, the habit which God made them to follow. And yet, says Jeremiah (8.7-8), men do not know their ordinance from the Lord. They were made to turn back to Him. *Mishpat* is therefore what God ordained. The basis is religious in the sense that it is of God. Whatever is revealed in life and custom of the way which God has ordained that men and living creatures generally should act, that is *mishpat*. God Himself is the norm. This is why the judgement of the Christian will on occasion vary from the judgement of even a good man. The good man will act after the pattern which is held to be sound and correct human behaviour. The Christian will act, God helping him, in such fashion as is a reflection in him of the ways of God. Perhaps when we all come to the Judgement Day there will be many surprises, since, as the Lord declared to Samuel, 'the Lord seeth not as man seeth; for man looketh on the outward appearance, but the Lord looketh on the heart' (I Samuel 16.7). In this matter of *mishpat*, therefore, treating men differently from what they deserve, offering a full and free forgiveness, is not an extra graciousness on the part of God, added because of necessity to a normal character of strict and impartial justice. It is the essence of His Nature. He was like that from the beginning. He did not first lay down ethical demands for Israel to fulfil, and then, when Israel failed and fell short, turn to them in graciousness with the offer of a new beginning. He was full of graciousness when He first called Israel out of Egypt, and full of graciousness all the time. He always was the Saviour God. In the actual sequence of events, He was first the Saviour God and afterwards the God who gave Israel the commandments, showing them the way in which they could continue to know His saving grace. It was not the case that Israel had to qualify for His bounty by keeping the commandments. Israel received His bounty in the first place before there were any commandments laid down which she must obey. Keeping the commandments was a condition of continuing to know the bounty of the Lord, but it was not an initial condition of first receiving His bounty. And in any case, all the time, both at the beginning and through to the end, humble service and obedience is required. There are many of us who hope that when it is our turn to stand before the Judgement throne of God, there will be very little said about justice and deserts, but a very great deal about forgiveness and mercy. Indeed, if we come before that throne in true humbleness and penitence, we have every reason to hope that this will be the case.

The most important of the four bridal gifts of Hosea
2.19 is *chesed*, translated in the Revised Version by 'loving
kindness'. Once more reference must be made to the rele-
vant article in the S.C.M. *Theological Word Book*, pp.
136f. Curiously, Hosea 2.19 is the one place, outside the
Psalms (twenty-three times), where Miles Coverdale used
the English phrase 'loving kindness' (his own invention).
The rendering favoured by the late Sir George Adam Smith
is 'leal-love'. This is because the word *chesed* came to be
used in Hebrew to represent the attitude which each party
to a covenant ought to maintain towards the other. It is
used in cases where there is a recognized tie between the
two parties, against *chen*, which is used when there is no
mutual obligation. There is therefore in the word an
idea of loyalty. The weakness of the rendering 'loving
kindness' is that it does not represent sufficiently the idea
of strength and persistence which is involved. In this
connection the case of Isaiah 40.6 is valuable, where the
Revised Version follows the Authorized Version and has
'goodliness'. All the translators in the ancient versions
have gone astray here, except only the Targum, which has
'strength'. The whole point of the passage is the con-
trast between the ephemeral nature of man and the absolute
reliability of the Word and the promises of God: 'All
flesh is grass, and all its *chesed* is like the wild flower . . .
the grass withereth, the flower fadeth, but the word of our
God shall stand for ever' (Isaiah 40.6-8). The word *chesed*
stands for God's steady, persistent love for the Israel of
His choice. It is the love that will not let us go, the love
that not all man's weakness and sinfulness and stubborn-
ness can destroy.

In the Septuagint the word is translated by *eleos* (pity),
and the influence of this rendering is to be seen in the

Vulgate *misericordia*. These are the renderings which have influenced the English translators in their renderings 'loving kindness', 'kindness' (Jeremiah 2.2) and 'mercy' (Hosea 6.6, Micah 6.8). This is how it came about that when they were faced with Isaiah 40.6 they were, like their predecessors, wholly at a loss, and, again like their predecessors, they had to adopt a rendering which has no shadow of justification whatever. In Hosea 2.19 we have the unusual (unique, apart from the Psalms) rendering 'loving kindness'. This is because the word 'mercy' has been retained to stand for the following word *rachamim* (compassions). Possibly he was coupling the four words together in pairs: righteousness and judgement, loving kindnesses and mercies. If this is the case, then already in Hosea the word *chesed* is being influenced by the necessities of the situation. Hosea realizes that God's steadfast love to a persistently wayward Israel involves mercies and loving kindnesses (i.e. acts of loving kindness) more than anything else. It is God's persistent covenant love for Israel that makes Him willing to allure Israel once more into the wilderness and to make a new beginning. Hosea's first reaction is that God has finished completely with Israel when the marriage covenant broke down, and that He has refused to have any further compassion on the Israelites (Hosea 1.6). Perhaps this is how Hosea felt at first about his wife, Gomer-bath-Diblaim, when he realized that she was so completely unfaithful to him. It would be very natural if this was indeed his first reaction. But, if he truly loved her, he would soon be wondering if there was anything he could do to restore the situation and create a new marriage, a new covenant instead of the old one which she had broken (cf. Jeremiah 31.32). And so, Hosea realized also that God's strong love for wayward Israel would not allow His compassion to disappear altogether, as is stated in Hosea 1.6 and again in 2.4. To this extent God's steadfast love, His *chesed*, for Israel must show itself mostly in loving kindnesses and in those mercies which haply will bring Israel once more into a covenant fellowship with Him. We get here the beginning of a development which reaches its climax in the New Testament *charis* (grace), that undeserved, unmerited favour by which God in the first place enables us to turn to Him and in the second place maintains us 'in Christ'.

This *chesed* is the centre and core of Hosea's message. He realized that it is the most significant element in the Nature of God. As we have pointed out above, and must continue to insist, other religions and many philosophies have pointed to a God of morality and of strict and stern justice. The prophets, Hosea the first of them and next to him Jeremiah, knew that if it had not been for God's *chesed*, the story of God's people would have ceased before it had begun. The distinctiveness of the religion of the prophets and of Christianity, which in its full development and characteristic emphasis is the successor of prophets like Hosea and Jeremiah, is to be found in this word *chesed*, this word which Hosea has made peculiarly his own. This is his great contribution to religion. As we have suggested before, he was followed by Jeremiah, who also emphasized the personal, intimate relationship between God and man, but went a stage further in that he realized the necessity of an individual relationship between God and man, apart from (or 'in addition to' or 'as a true basis of') a national or group relationship (Jeremiah 31.31-34).

The fourth bridal gift is *rachamim* (mercies). This word is discussed in the S.C.M. *Theological Word Book,* pp. 143f. It is there stated that it has nothing to do with forgiveness of sin, except accidentally. It expressed the tender compassion of God, that pity which He has for us in all our troubles, especially in regard to the weakness of our human nature and frame. The typical passage, in which the cognate verb is used (translated 'pity' in the Revised Version) is Psalm 103.13-14. 'Like as a father pitieth his children, so the Lord pitieth them that fear him. For he knoweth our frame; He remembereth that we are dust.' The importance of the word here in Hosea, in Hosea 2.19 in particular and in the whole of Hosea's message in general, is that it shows the way in which God's *chesed* became more than faithfulness in the original covenant. His 'pity' for human nature generally, and especially His greater compassion for the people whom He loved and called out of Egypt, were the cause of that initiative of God's whereby there is any chance at all of a new and second covenant. This difference in knowledge of the ways of God with Israel springs from the way in which Hosea approached the whole matter. There was little chance of this discovery being made by a man like Amos who thought of God primarily as the stern hard God of the desert. It was given to Hosea, through his own bitter personal experiences, to realize that personal relationship which is the key to the understanding of the Nature of God.

We have spoken all along of God's initiative, of God choosing Israel in the first place and taking the initiative in rescuing Israel from Egypt to be a son, and then, when Israel turned away and broke the old covenant, of God once more taking the initiative in seeking to institute a new covenant. Hosea's attitude is that Israel herself is unable of herself to turn to God. This is not as prominent in Hosea as it is elsewhere, but it is involved in Hosea 5.4 and again in 11.7.

The actual translation of Hosea 5.4 is uncertain, though the general meaning of the verse is plain enough. It reads, either: 'They will not (or 'can not') frame their doings so as to return to their God' or: 'Their doings will not allow them to return to their God.' If we read 'can not' in the first alternative, then in either case we have an Israel unable to turn. Happily the latter part of the verse makes this meaning quite clear: 'Because a *ruach* ('spirit') of whoredom is in their midst and they do not know the Lord.' This is comparable to Hosea 4.12: 'Because a *ruach* of whoredom has led them astray, and they have gone awhoring from under their God', a metaphor which is crude but expressive.

The important word in these verses is the word *ruach*, translated 'spirit'. The word is used here in a semi-psychological sense, and it denotes that which dominates the whole man to the exclusion of anything else. For a full examination of this Old Testament use, see the first essay in *The Doctrine of the Holy Spirit*.[1] One of the most illuminating examples is to be found in Numbers 5.14 and 30, in the passage which lays down the procedure for a man to follow if he suspects his wife's fidelity. The law says that 'if a *ruach* of jealousy come upon a man . . .', he must do this and that and so forth. The idea is of an overmastering, all-compelling influence coming upon the man, so strong that he is helpless against it. Jealousy is like that, and anyone who has had to deal with a jealous man or woman knows how utterly impossible it is to drive any sense into them. They are definitely under control, under complete control of some other power. The sickness of melancholia is another example, and other kinds of ill-ness also where the sufferers are conscious of some great

[1] The Headingley Lectures, 2nd edition, 1941.

blanket of depression settling over them, with a blackness
and an inevitability that will not be denied. There are
some thirty-five or so cases in the Old Testament where
the word *ruach* is used in this way. When, therefore,
Hosea says that ' a *ruach* of whoredoms ' has led the people
astray, he is thinking of them as being helpless in the
grip of a power which they cannot withstand. Both in
Hosea 4.12 and in Hosea 11.7, therefore, the prophet is
speaking of Israel as being unable—possibly willing, possibly unwilling, but certainly unable to turn back to
God.

It was this inability to turn back to God which puzzled
Jeremiah (8.4-7). He saw the migratory birds of Palestine
(the stork, the turtle-dove, the swallow and the crane) come
back regularly every year, fulfilling their natural habits.
It is their *mishpat* (translated ' ordinance ' in 8.7, with
' judgement ' in the margin, as in the text of Authorized
Version). The point of the word is that they are following their ' habit ', their inherited custom, the thing which,
as migratory birds, they were made to do. Man's *mishpat*
is to turn back to God, but he does not do it, this thing
he was made to do. Jeremiah's solution is to be found in
Jeremiah 31.31-34, in that new heart which God will
implant in every man. Hosea has found the solution in
part, because he realizes that if the new covenant is going
to stand the slightest chance of being even established,
then God will have to give Israel those qualities of heart and
mind which are essential. So we get Hosea 2.19 with its
talk of the betrothal gift which the bridegroom will give
to the bride : *tsedeq, mishpat, chesed* and *rachamim*; i.e.
a modelling of her conduct on what he knows to be the
nature of God, a following of her true destiny in doing
what she was made to do, a new steadfastness and loyalty,

and that compassion which is the outcome of true loving kindness.

This idea of *ruach* as a dominating power is important for the proper understanding of the New Testament doctrine of the Holy Spirit. Its precursor in the Old Testament is the *ruach adonai*, the spirit of the Lord, a power from outside the man himself, a more-than-human power which enables a man to do what of himself and in his own strength, he is unable to do. This compelling, enabling power is to be seen at its crudest in the stories of Samson, the Trickster of Hebrew folklore. By it he is able to perform most extraordinary feats of strength (Judges 13.25, 14.6 and 19, 15.14). The feats vary in usefulness and in moral value, but they are unfailingly marvellous and out of the ordinary. Or again, it is when the spirit of the Lord comes lightly upon Saul that he is 'turned into another man', and does things which normally he never did, so that men were astonished and said: 'Is Saul also among the prophets?' (I Samuel 10.6 and 10.11). The skilled craftsman, Bezalel ben Uri, was divinely called to make the furniture of the Tent of Meeting, assisted by Oholiab ben Ahisamach and others. But in order to make all these things, he was 'filled . . . with the spirit of God, in wisdom, and in understanding, and in knowledge, and in all manner of workmanship' in order to perform all sorts of skilled work in gold, silver, bronze, cutting of gems, and wood-carving. His skill was supernatural skill, more even than human genius developed by excellent training. He was possessed by an outside, enabling power, the *ruach* of God. The crown of this development in the Old Testament is to be seen in Micah 3.8: 'But truly I am full of power, even the spirit of the Lord, and of judgement, and of might, to declare unto Jacob his rebellion and unto Israel his sin.' Here, as also in Nehemiah 9.30, the spirit of the Lord is that power which inspired the prophets and made them different from other men.

Once more we get a difference due to a Hebrew background as against the classical background. The tendency of the classical tradition is to think of all inspiration as due to the Holy Spirit, but not to the Holy Spirit as a more-than-human power which invades men, changes them, and enables them to do more-than-human things. The tendency is to think of such inspiration as the highest form of human endeavour, man's own spirit at its noblest and best, the *logos spermatikos* in its purest form. If we work from a Hebrew background, we think of God the Holy Spirit as wholly different from the human spirit, the very power of God in man, transforming him and enabling him to fulfil God's will in a way which is not possible for him otherwise to do.

V

SACRIFICE AND THE PROPHETS

ONE of the best-known passages in Hosea is to be found in Hosea 6.6: 'For I desire *chesed* ('mercy') and not sacrifice; and the knowledge of God more than burnt-offerings.' The importance of the verse lies partly in the problem of the attitude of the canonical prophets to the ritual of shrine and temple, but partly also to the fact that our Lord is twice reported to have quoted the verse, each time in defence of the breaking of the rules of the orthodox religious behaviour of the day. In the one instance (Matthew 9.13) He Himself was the offender in that He was eating with publicans and sinners, outcasts from everything that had to do with the Temple worship because they did not fulfil the strict laws which governed ritual cleanness. In the other case, His disciples were the offenders because they had plucked the ears of corn, rubbed them in their hands to thresh them and had eaten the grains, all on the day of the Sabbath (Matthew 12.7). In addition to these definite quotations, there is also the reply of the scribe who had asked which was the greatest commandment of all. The scribe had welcomed our Lord's quotations from Deuteronomy 6.4-6 and Leviticus 19.18, and he declared (with a reminiscence of Hosea 6.6) that loving God with all the heart and loving one's neighbour as oneself is 'much more than all whole burnt-offerings and sacrifices' (Mark 12.33). Our Lord's answer was: 'Thou art not far from the kingdom of God,' so it is evident that such sentiments met with His fullest approval.

What then was the attitude of the canonical prophets to that offering of sacrifices which later formed the main element in the Temple ritual and became the corner-stone of the Jewish religious structure?

It seems to be plain that both Amos (5.25) and Jeremiah (7.22) were of the opinion that there were no sacrifices in the desert in the days before Israel entered Canaan. The question which Amos asks ('Did ye bring me sacrifices and offerings in the wilderness forty years, O house of Israel?') clearly from the context expects the answer 'No'. Jeremiah roundly declares that God issued no instructions in the desert on these matters: 'For I spake not unto your fathers, nor commanded them in the day that I brought them out of the land of Egypt, concerning burnt offerings or sacrifices.' They may have been right or they may have been wrong (that is another matter), but this is what they thought and said.

Amos refers to two types of offerings, the *zebach* and the *minchah*. The *zebach* was at all periods of Hebrew history a slaughtered beast of which the larger part was eaten by those whose offering it was. The word etymologi-cally means 'slaughtered thing'. According to Leviticus 3.1-17, the blood was to be sprinkled all round the altar, and all the fat, together with the kidneys and the caudate lobe which grows out from the liver, was to be burned up in smoke on the altar as 'a sweet savour unto the Lord'. This passage, it is true, is to be found in the Priestly Code, but many of the details found there are of very ancient origin, and it is extremely likely that many of them remained unchanged during the centuries. The rest of the

animal, apart from the parts detailed above, was, in post-
exilic times, eaten by the worshippers at the Temple during
a sacred meal. In the pre-Deuteronomic period, the ceremonies described in Leviticus 3.1-17 may well have taken
place in respect of every slaughtered beast at the local
shrine. That is, the blood was probably drained out and
'given' to the God, possibly the fat was extracted also
for the Deity, whilst the remainder may either have been
eaten at the shrine (on special occasions and high holy
days) or have been taken home and eaten there. We know
that a distinction had to be made in the Deuteronomic
legislation between killing for food at home and killing
for the holy meal at the Single Sanctuary (Deuteronomy
12.20-28), so presumably there was only one type of killing
before that time. It was the establishment of the Single
Sanctuary which caused the difficulty. This could only
be because men could not travel so far every time they
wanted to eat meat for their dinner, so, presumably, before
Josiah's time all slaughter was at the local shrine because
of the necessity of dealing adequately and correctly with
the blood.

The other sacrifice which Amos mentions was the
minchah. This was in pre-exilic times a gift to God of
any type. The word itself means 'tribute', cf. I Kings
4.21, where the usual translation is 'presents'. The
minchah was a gift to God at the shrine, as if to a king.
None of it reverted in any way to the worshipper. In
the post-exilic period, that is according to the Priestly Code,
the *minchah* was the cereal offering which accompanied
every meat offering that was burned on the altar.

Amos held that there were no *zebachs* and no *minchahs*
in the wilderness. These two types include all the sacrifices of pre-exilic days. Jeremiah's statement has the same

significance. The terms he uses are *zebach* and *'olah*, the former, as we have seen, largely eaten by the worshipper, the latter wholly burned on the altar. Thus both Amos and Jeremiah completely rule out any sacrifice for the period of the wanderings in the wilderness.

If this is indeed what these two prophets meant, were they right? They may both have been mistaken, sincere though they both undoubtedly were.

All the evidence we have points to the conclusion that the three great feasts, all three of which were harvest festivals, were Canaanite in origin. The Hebrews knew nothing of them before they entered Canaan. The three harvest festivals are the Barley Harvest Festival (Unleavened Bread), that of the wheat (Weeks, later Pentecost), and that of the vintage and everything else (Ingathering: after the exile, split into the three festivals of Tishri). They were all pilgrimages, since a harvest festival necessarily involves a journey to a shrine. The first-fruits must be brought to the holy place. Since, therefore, the three great feasts were all based on the agriculture of Canaan, Amos and Jeremiah were certainly right so far as these celebrations and the sacrifices connected with them are concerned. There were no such feasts in the desert, and no such ritual and sacrifices.

It is true that in Deuteronomy 16.3 the eating of un-leavened cakes is explained with reference to the haste with which the ancestors of the Israelites came out of Egypt, and that there is also an explanation, though far from clear, for the Feast of Weeks as being connected with the Egyptian slavery. On the other hand there is no such explanation given for the Feast of Tabernacles (Deuteronomy 16.13-17), which is the post-exilic name for those elements of the pre-exilic autumnal feast which clung to the harvest full moon when the calendar was changed at the exile. The desert explanation for the living in booths (tabernacles) appears as late as Nehemiah 8.13-17, though there is no doubt about this living in booths for the period of the feast being an old vintage custom. Further, in Leviticus 23, which seems to be the basis of the post-exilic regulations concerning the festivals and the feasts, there are no explanations offered which provide associations with the wilderness, and the same is true of the pre-exilic regulations found in Exodus 23.14-16, with the exception of the phrase in verse 15, evidently realized by the English translators to be out of construction because of the brackets: 'for in it (i.e. in the month Abib) thou camest out of Egypt'. The explanations which connect the harvest festivals with the rescue from Egypt and the subsequent period in the wilderness are later interpretations. They grow as the generations come and go, and they are part of the deliberate way in which Israel linked up everything with the saving work of God, continually emphasizing this foundation of both nation and religion.

Apart from all this, the very nature of the three harvest festivals ties them down to an agricultural community. They belong to the ways of a settled people, not of nomads. They are tied, not only to an agricultural people, but to an agricultural year. Because of this they have no point of contact with a desert people such as Israel was before the entrance into Canaan. The only rite known to the Israelites before they entered Canaan was the Passover rite. This was never a shrine or temple rite, but always essentially belonging to the home. In the days of the Second Temple, the Passover lambs were slain in the temple and the blood was poured out at the altar, but all the rest of the Passover ritual was away from the Temple in the 'home', whether the actual home of the participants or a hired room which would satisfy the regulations as being a home 'within the meaning of the act'. Orginally the Passover was an apotropaic rite, that is, a rite for the turning away of evil spirits, but it was transformed by Hebrew religious genius, even before the entrance into Canaan, into the annual commemoration of the rescue from Egypt. In the last days of Herod's Temple it became virtually the Feast of the Coming of Messiah, who should rescue his people from the Roman bondage just as Moses had been God's instrument in rescuing their fathers from the Egyptian bondage.

On the other hand, there were certainly *zebach*s in the days before the Hebrews came across Jordan into Canaan, because the *zebach*, as the word itself implies, was originally the ordinary killing of a beast for food. There was no association in those days with any shrine. We may safely assume that the sort of thing which happened in the desert was similar to the action of Saul as described in I Samuel 14.34. In the previous verse, we are told that the victorious but very hungry Israelites captured the sheep and oxen of the defeated Philistines, and set to work straight away to satisfy their ravenous hunger. They killed the beasts straight away where they were and ate the carcases, blood and flesh together. Saul was horrified when he heard what they were doing. He bade his informants roll a great stone to where he was. Then he told them to order all the people to bring their beasts to him so that they could be slaughtered properly. He slaughtered them on the stone, which thus became 'a place of slaughter', *mizbeach*, which is the regular Hebrew word for 'altar'. We thus see what was the origin of the altar amongst the Hebrews. It was originally the stone on which the actual

killing was done. When Saul had drained out the blood
over the stone, the flesh was free from tabu and safe to be
eaten. As we have seen, the distinction between killing
for food and killing for a sacred meal at the Single Sanctuary came in with the centralization of the Deuteronomic
reforms (Deuteronomy 12.15-16).

We judge therefore that Amos and Jeremiah were not
denying that there was any 'sacrifice' in the desert, since
men must eat flesh in the desert or starve. They were not
denying, that is, that the blood of a slaughtered beast was
'poured out unto the Lord'. On the other hand, when
they say that there were no *minchah*s (tribute-offerings) or
'*olah*s in the desert, they are denying that the nomad
Israelites gave gifts to God, gifts of kind, first-fruits or
tithes and such like. The first impulse is hotly to deny
the truth of such a suggestion, but it must be remembered
that amongst many peoples of an undeveloped stage in
society, there are no sacrifices made to the High God, and
no prayers offered to Him. Again and again, when we read
accounts of the worship of early peoples, we find that all
rites and ceremonies belong to the cults of the 'low gods',
those nearer deities who are supposed to control the immediate affairs of men. It may well be that there were no
gift-offerings to God in the pre-Canaanite Hebrew religion.
In this case Amos was right in saying that there were no
*minchah*s in those days, and Jeremiah was right in saying
that there were no commandments concerning '*olah*s.

Against this, the natural reply is to quote the story of
the gifts brought by the two brothers, Cain and Abel,
recounted in Genesis 4.3-5. But even there we find something curious about the use of the word *minchah*. Cain's
gift, which was the gift of the agriculturalist, is called a
minchah throughout the story. But Abel's gift, the gift

of the nomad, is at first (verse 4) said to be 'from the first-lings of his flock'. Later on, in verse 5, the offerings of both brothers are referred to as *minchah*s. The use of the term is too vague for any safe conclusion to be drawn, though, according to pre-exilic terminology, an offering of first-fruits might possibly be called a *minchah*, in the sense of a tribute-offering. On the other hand, if *minchah* should be taken to mean 'gift', then the word cannot be used of first-fruits, because first-fruits are in no sense a gift to the deity. The whole theory of first-fruits is against this. The theory is that all produce of every kind belongs to the God, whether produce of field, or fold, or even man and woman. Everything that is produced, whether grown or born, is God's; it is *qodesh*, 'holy' in the sense of belonging to God and therefore tabu to man. But man must bring the first-fruits to God at His shrine and present them before God. These God accepts. Man can redeem by payment of an equivalent the first-born of animals and birds. If he does not redeem the first-born of a she-ass, the ass-foal must be strangled. In all these cases, man has a choice. But he must redeem his own first-born. The details are to be found in Exodus 13.11-13 and 15, also 34.19-20.

Amos and Jeremiah are evidently speaking against the whole system of sacrifices as they knew them at the shrines of Canaan, wherever the Israelites had taken over the cult of the Canaanites. The cutting-edge of their sayings is directed against the only cult they know, the cult as followed by the Israelites in Canaan, a cult which was almost wholly if not entirely Canaanite and pagan in origin.

Isaiah's tirade against the sacrifices is to be found in chapter 1.11-15. He roundly condemns every type of pre-exilic sacrifice, and every type of festival—new months, sabbaths, calling of convocations (probably the three great pilgrimage feasts), fasts (following the Greek, instead of the 'iniquity' of the Hebrew text), closing assemblies ('solemn meeting' in the English Versions). Isaiah says that God hates the whole system from start to finish. It is a burden to Him and He cannot stand it any longer. He will not listen to their prayers: in short, He will have nothing to do with any part or aspect of their worship. But Isaiah continues with a call to repentance. When he says that God will not listen to the prayers they offer with outstretched hands, he says also that their hands are covered with blood (verse 15). He bids them wash and be clean, put away their evil deeds so that He cannot see them, repent, mend their ways, and see that the father-less children and the widows get true justice. There are two possibilities here. Perhaps Isaiah is wholly against the temple system of his day; or perhaps he is against the system as they adhere to it on the ground of the wicked-ness of the daily lives of the worshippers. The latter is the more likely though certainty is impossible. It is true that Isaiah received his call as a prophet whilst he was in the temple during the offering of the sacrifices (Isaiah 6.4, ? the reference to the smoke). This, however, may mean no more than that he was actually there, as a matter of fact, when he received his call. Possibly he may have changed his mind later about the efficacy or the desira-bility of sacrifices. There is no evidence either way. On the other hand, we can see even in his account of his call, the same consciousness of the wickedness of a people who say one thing with their lips in the temple (verse 5) and do something quite different with their whole lives out-side in the city. The same conclusion must therefore be drawn from Isaiah 6.1-6 as from Isaiah 1.10-17, which is that Isaiah is objecting to the sacrifices of his day on the ground of the wickedness and insincerity of the worshippers.

And so we come back again to Hosea 6.6, which has substantially the same message as Micah 6.6-8. Hosea puts *zebachs* (eaten by the worshippers) and *'olahs* (wholly burned on the altar) into one category, and he puts *chesed* ('loving kindness') and 'knowledge of God' into another category. He makes no declaration as to whether sacrifices are right or wrong, but he leaves us in no shadow of doubt as to which, in his opinion, God prefers. God puts true piety and knowledge of Himself first, and as the scribe said to our Lord many hundreds of years afterwards, loving God and one's neighbour is more than all burnt-offerings and sacrifices. For this, as we have seen, Jesus commended him as He commended very few.

Hosea 3.4 is usually brought forward as evidence that Hosea was in favour of sacrifices, and not only of sacrifices but of all sorts of temple furniture—pillars, ephods, terephini and so forth, enough paraphernalia to satisfy even the most ardent pre-Deuteronomic anti-reformationist. It is held that Hosea thought it would be a punishment for Israel to be in exile without king, prince, sacrifice and the rest. This is the usual interpretation of Hosea 3.4, but we have suggested above (p. 50) that in our judgement the whole chapter is late and that none of it can be ascribed to Hosea. The problem is, as we have indicated, a double one. First, the woman of chapter 3 is already a harlot, and so can scarcely be Gomer-bath-Diblaim. The easiest explanation is that another writer is at work who is using Hosea's original allegory and is taking Hosea 1.2 to mean that Gomer was a harlot from the beginning of the story. Second, there is the difficulty of deciding where the addi-

D

tion to chapter 3 begins. The usual opinion is that the
addition begins with 'and David their king'. But if we
take the whole chapter as an addition, we have a Judaean
writer of a post-Deuteronomic age, rejoicing that Israel, the
northern kingdom, who served other gods (note that the
word is 'gods' and not the 'the baalim', which is what
Hosea usually says, whereas 'other gods' is the usual
Deuteronomic phrase for the Canaanite deities), are stripped
of their irregular non-Davidic kings and princes, and
stripped also of all the adjuncts to that irregular worship
which the southerners held to be 'the sin wherewith
Jeroboam son of Nebat made them to sin'. Then it is
that the Israelites of the north will come back again to the
Lord their God, back to Jerusalem to the One Sanctuary,
and back to the Davidic king. All will then be well 'in
the latter days'.

Our conclusion in respect of Hosea is that he is against
the sacrifices he knew, not necessarily on the ground that
they were sacrifices of one type and another, but on the
ground of the wickedness of those that brought them.
The other passages referring to *zebach*s confirm this:
Hosea 8.13, 9.4.

The passage in Jeremiah which we have discussed (7.22)
falls into line with the rest. Jeremiah denies that God
gave commands in the wilderness concerning the different
types of sacrifices, but he goes on to specify the commands
which God did give. These commands are not specified
in detail, but they are included in a call for right living.
Nevertheless, it remains true that Jeremiah pays the mini-
mum of reverence to the temple and its sacrifices. He says
(7.21) that for all God cares they can eat the *'olah*s as well
as the *zebach*s, and, so to speak, much good may they
do them. That is, they can eat not only those sacrifices

which it is proper for the worshippers to eat, but that they can eat up those which properly belong to God; none of them are more than flesh which men eat. Earlier in the chapter, Jeremiah is speaking against the temple. It is not the slightest use for them to cling to the temple (7.4), pinning their faith to it and to what goes on there. It has become nothing other than a den of thieves (7.11). Scholars have held that in verse 3 Jeremiah is promising that the temple will not be destroyed if the people amend their ways and deeds. Presumably this interpretation is based on the assumption that ' this place ' means the temple. But the natural meaning here of the word ' place ' is Palestine. The verse means that God will permit the people to remain in the Promised Land and that He will not cast them out. Compare the meaning of the word in 7.14, 7.20, and so generally, 19.12, etc.; though, of course, there are cases where ' place ' means the temple. Jeremiah evidently had little use for the temple and what went on there. We have to remember that Jeremiah was ' of the priests that were in Anathoth ' (Jeremiah 1.1), and that therefore he was probably a descendant of the ancient priesthood of Shiloh, guardians of the Ark from the days of Egypt (I Samuel 2.27-28). He cannot therefore be expected to show much sympathy with them and their ritual, especially in view of Jeremiah 8.8 and II Kings 23.9, passages which may be taken as evidence that the Zadokite priests of Jerusalem used the Deuteronomic reforms to their own advantage. Doubtless all that Jeremiah has to say about sacrifices has to be placed against this background. Whether he was right or wrong is another matter; the fact that he was a non-Zadokite and that the rapacious priests of Jerusalem were Zadokites, wholly exclusive and thieves and robbers, explains how he came to his conclusions.

There is little evidence of the attitude of Ezekiel to the sacrificial system. His picture of what went on in the temple in the last days is not very encouraging (Ezekiel 8). No one could have many regrets for its destruction and the cessation of sacrifice, that is if they have any desire for worship that is true and pure. The last nine chapters of the Book of the Prophet Ezekiel form a blueprint for the days of restoration. There seems to be no particular evidence that they are by Ezekiel himself (whoever Ezekiel was). They appear to be of Zadokite inspiration, establishing the Zadokites in the dominant position in the new city-state, which their behaviour in respect of the Deuteronomic reformation leads us to expect of them. Nor is there any evidence that Ezekiel was a priest, apart from the editorial Ezekiel 1.3 and the fact that the last nine chapters are where they are.

It is best to place the two extremists on one side, Jeremiah and the writer of Ezekiel 40-48, and to address ourselves to the prophets who take up a more central position. It cannot be said with truth that any of them were enthusiastic on behalf of sacrifices. Judging from the evidence they have left behind, the most that can be said is that they were very sure that there was something else which is much more acceptable to God. To Hosea, this something else was *chesed* and knowledge of God; that is, faithfulness and that knowledge of the will of God which shows itself chiefly in the avoidance of such human conduct as is listed in Hosea 4.2: breaking oaths, murder, theft and adultery. Hosea says that if only the priests (4.5-9) had done their full duty and had taught God's people what is God's law, there would have been a very different story to tell. Sacrifices are worse than useless if they are not backed by true living. They are worse than useless

(Isaiah 1.17) if they are not backed by that care for those that have no helper which is essential to the prophetic idea of 'righteousness'. Israel must be loyal and faithful to God. Israel must conform to that pattern of conduct which is in accordance with His nature. Such faithfulness and loyalty is more than all sacrifices. In so far as sacrifices are the outward expression of true thankfulness of heart and true repentance, they are acceptable to God. Otherwise He hates them; they are an abomination to Him. The essence of religion, therefore, according to these prophets, is not in sacrifices, however many and however splendid. It is in true repentance and in the fulfilment of those principles of conduct which are well pleasing to Him.

Further, the prophets have managed to cut loose from the ancient idea that sacrifices in themselves are effective. The idea of the efficacy of sacrificial rites in particular or ritual acts in general has been the curse of religion.

VI

THE VALUE OF SACRIFICE

IF, THEN, these prophets who were the glory of Israel, were either flatly against sacrifices, or at least viewed them with apprehension and concern, what is the value of sacrifice? Is there any need for it? Is there any justification or any wisdom in associating the life and death of our Lord with the idea of sacrifice? What is the meaning of the word 'sacrifice'?

It is important in the first place that the English word 'sacrifice' should be carefully and closely defined. One of the difficulties in discussions concerning sacrifice in general or the Atonement in particular is caused by the loose use of the word 'sacrifice'. Writers tend to start with one meaning for the word, and to finish with another. The word 'sacrificial' has a host of meanings in our English tongue, and many of those who use the word are not careful enough of their exact meaning. This wide variation in the use of words is the danger and difficulty of most discussions, whatever the subject under discussion. Words have a broad front rather than a pin point, and one writer may be thinking of a right-wing meaning whilst another thinks of a left-wing meaning. Further, each writer is liable to move along his front from wing and centre, or, perhaps, under the stress of argument, from centre to wing, quite unconscious that he has varied at all in his use of the term. The fallacy of 'the undistributed middle' trips us all up as soon as our zeal in defence of any position interferes with the cold detachment of academic discussion. Added to this is the fact that, except for an isolated few, anything that is worth discussing, is also worth a zealous defence. If we could always remember that all the words we use are metaphors, and that as soon as we move away from the object to which the word is properly attached, the word has to be used with particular care, we might save ourselves a great deal of confusion. We are indeed allowed, within sensible limits, to be like Humpty-Dumpty and to make a word mean just what we choose it to mean, but having done this, we must follow Humpty-Dumpty to the end, and remember that he concluded by saying 'neither more nor less'.

The English word 'sacrifice' is an anglicized form of the Latin *sacrificium*. Our difficulty does not arise from the use of the Latin word itself, which is fairly solidly used in the sense of a victim slain and wholly consumed on the altar. The difficulty lies in the varied uses of the English word, some of which go back to the strict derivative meaning of the Latin word, whilst other uses are so figurative as to mean the offering of almost anything—prayer, thanksgiving, penitence, submission, and so forth (see the Oxford dictionary). The strict derivative meaning of the Latin *sacrificium* is 'to make *sacer*', that is, to bring something or someone within the realm or orbit of the *sacer*. This latter word concerns that which is consecrated or belongs to a divinity, that which is 'holy'. Thus, in its strictest sense, the word *sacrificium* is concerned with that which is brought or has come to be within the sphere of holy things, and it may refer to any action in the cultus, or any thing or person connected with the shrine or the

Deity. The word may be used in the sense of the Greek *thusia*, an offering (properly one that has been slain) either public or private, though even as early as Homer this word *thusia* is used in the sense of 'sacred rites' generally. Or again, the word may be used in the sense of the Greek *prosphora*, that which is brought as a present, a gift, though here again we have the difficulty of a wide meta-phorical use of the word. Thus, the English word 'sacrifice' can be used of killing something (though not neces-sarily in a religious association), of giving something, of giving up something, or, religiously, of performing an act in the cultus, at a shrine or in the home, though not necessarily killing anything or even giving anything. When the word is used without careful definition, the discussion is apt to become confusing because of all this varied use.

The kind of confusion we get can be seen, for instance, in the late Professor W. O. E. Oesterley's *Sacrifices in Ancient Israel*, p. 12. He says that 'the term " sacrifice " is somewhat misleading when used in reference to the offerings of uncultured peoples; . . . it connotes, in its modern use, something made holy, i.e. something forfeited or destroyed, and by that act dedicated to the Deity'. Whether this statement would satisfy us all is much open to question, but Dr. Oesterley was, at any rate, saying clearly what he himself meant by that modern use of the word. But he goes on to say that 'to early man an offering did not partake of a holy character, at any rate in the modern sense'. By this he appears to mean that early man's offerings were utilitarian: 'he gave in order to receive, for the most part . . . egotism entered in to a large extent.' It is probable that such a test as this would eliminate a great deal of what passes in modern times for 'sacrifice' in holy things. We judge that by 'sacrifice', Dr. Oesterley meant 'holy sacrifice', and that by 'holy' he meant moral, or better still, altruistic. He concludes the paragraph by saying that we have become so accustomed to using the term in its non-etymological sense that there is no objection to our using the term in reference to savages. This is confusing. It seems to us that Dr. Oesterley was using the word in a non-etymological sense when he used the word 'holy' in the sense of moral and altruistic, and that it is precisely this modern use of the term which makes it inapplicable to the offerings of savages.

If we think of the original meaning of *sacer*, there is no difficulty in thinking of the rites of early man as sacrifices, since, as Rudolf Otto has shown in his *The Idea of the Holy*, the word *sacer* (English 'holy', Hebrew *qodesh*) had originally no moral or altruistic meaning. It meant originally that which has to do with the otherness of things, that non-visible, supra-human world with which early man believed himself to be on every side surrounded. Otto used the word 'numinous' for this element in human experience, this awareness, that is, of an outside non-human world. Its main constituent is creature-feeling, with its sense of a *mysterium tremendum*, the *mysterium* referring to the Wholly Other, and the elements of *tremendum* being awefulness, overpoweringness and urgency. There is nothing here at this stage of morality and altruism. What early man offered or did was exactly a sacrifice, nothing more and nothing less. His action had to do with the numinous, and it was all concerned with that which has to do with the more-than-human. The early Hebrew use of the word *qodesh* gives exactly the sense required, since from its earliest known stages *qodesh* means that which has to do with Deity. The developing content of *qodesh*

in the Old Testament goes hand in hand with the developing knowledge of God, so that whatever at any stage God
is known to be, that is *qodesh*. Thus, to say that God is
qadosh ('holy', the adjective) is to make a statement which
has no meaning; the meaning of *qadosh* is conditioned by
what we know about God. This should be true about the
English word 'holy', if, that is, we are to be influenced
by the biblical use of the word. Most modern ideas of
'holy' are inadequate and sub-Christian. The word is
usually taken to mean 'moral purity' or the like; it refers
to some standard which has come down to us by way of
the classical tradition. For the Christian who has not been
brought up under the influence of those Greek-Latin traditions which even Sanday and Headlam viewed with sus-
picion, the word 'holy' signifies first and foremost all
that can be said concerning the Saviour God, this God
who demands from His worshippers a righteousness which
not only exceeds that of the scribes, but that of the best
of the Greeks and Romans also.

Turning to the idea of sacrifice as referring to an object
that is brought to the shrine, there are three main aspects
involved. In practice it may be that, as often as not, the
various aspects are confused, but from the point of view
of analysis and for the sake of clarity, it is essential that
they are kept distinct. The three main aspects of sacrifice
are gift, expiation, means of communion. Further, the
word used to denote the type of sacrificial offering depends
in some cases on the intention with which the offering is
brought, and in other cases upon what is done with the
offering after it has been brought.

First, the aspect of a sacrifice as a gift.

(*a*) The object may be brought as a gift as to a king,
in homage and as an acknowledgement of his superiority

and his right to loyalty. This is the Hebrew *minchah* of pre-exilic times. As we have seen, the word *minchah* strictly means ' homage '. What happened to the gift after it had been brought was, in pre-exilic times, of little importance. There does not appear to have been a word in regular use related to the subsequent treatment of the gift. Whatever happened to it afterwards it was a *minchah* because it was brought as a tribute-gift to the King-God. The offering might be wholly consumed on the altar, that is, burned up in smoke so that the Deity could partake of it. This idea can still be traced in the Old Testament where God is referred to as refusing to smell an offering. The classical expression for such ideas is to be found in the old Babylonian flood-story, in the description of the sacrifice which the Babylonian Noah offers after his deliverance from the Flood. The gods are described as smelling the goodly savour, and gathering like flies over the sacrificer. The gift-offering which was wholly consumed on the altar was, at all periods, called an ' *olah* (' burnt-offering '). Since in post-exilic times the *minchah* was the cereal-offering which accompanied every whole burnt-offering, it is possible that in pre-exilic times the term tended rather to be concerned with such gifts as did not go to the altar. These other gifts went to the maintenance of the personnel, the priests and the various other attendants at the shrine, or for the general service of the temple. In later, i.e. post-exilic times, a gift which was allocated to the use of the temple personnel was included under the general title of *qodashim* (' holy things ', Numbers 18.8-32). This term included everything that came to the priest, whatever its origin. It included the share of the priest who performed whatever ceremonies had to be performed. It included both the ' heave-offering ' (that which the priest lifted up with a vertical motion) and the 'wave-offering' (that which the priest took and presented by moving the portion to and fro horizontally). It included the allocated portion of all slaughtered animals, whether they were destined to be consumed completely on the altar (whole burnt-offerings), or whether they were intended to provide a holy meal for the worshippers. The term included every type of first-fruits, not because it was a first-fruit, but because it went to the service of the priesthood.

On the other hand, gifts which were allocated to the service of the sanctuary, as distinct from the maintenance of the temple personnel, came under the general head of *qorbanim*. This included whatever was consumed in smoke on the altar as well as whatever was allocated to the service and furnishing of the temple.

(*b*) The gift may be brought as a payment under a *métayage* system. This is a system which developed as a first stage from serfdom in Flanders and in Central Italy (*mezzandria* system) towards the end of the thirteenth century, whereby the owner let his estate to tenants who paid rent by giving to the landowner a proportion of the harvest or of the stock in kind. It is analogous to the share-crop system of the prairies. All first-fruits come under this head. There are two classes of first-fruits, *bikkurim* and *re'shith*. The *bikkurim* included the first-fruits of wheat, barley, the vine, figs, pomegranates, olives and honey. All other first-fruits were *re'shith*. The theory of first-fruits is that all produce of every kind belongs to God, whether of field or fold, or the offspring of men and women themselves. The first-fruits (first-born) must be brought to God, and presented to Him. The first-born of cattle may be redeemed on payment of the redemption value; the first-born of an ass must be either redeemed or strangled; the first-born of man must be redeemed. Those first-fruits which are not redeemed are *qodashim*, because they become the perquisite of the priests.

(c) The gift may be brought in order to feed and keep alive the Deity. This, according to Herbert Spencer, is the origin of sacrifice. It involved primarily the leaving of food and drink at the graves of the dead in order to refresh the ancestral spirits. When these ancestral spirits (so Herbert Spencer) rose to divine rank, the gifts became sacrifices. Here we are involved in Herbert Spencer's theories of the development of religion. The archæological evidence from Palestine suggests that in early times food and drink were deposited by the graves of the departed, but whether this has any connection with such sacrifices as are mentioned in the Old Testament, is very doubtful indeed. There is a growing belief that the monotheism of the Old Testament did not develop out of animism, fetichism, worship of ancestral spirits, and the like, but that it was due to a direct revelation independent of all this worship of 'low gods'. But the origin of the drink-offering was probably to feed the Deity, whether it was a pouring out of water to the Lord or the water and wine of the drink-offerings of the post-exilic temple. Possibly this also is why the blood of slain beasts were poured at the foot of the altar, or that of birds spattered against it. And it may be also that those sacrifices which were gifts to God (whole burnt-offerings and the parts of others which were burned in smoke on the altar) were also intended to feed the Deity with food that had been made *qodosh* (holy).

(d) The fourth type of gift was that which was made with the intention of placating the Deity. The origin of such gifts is said by adherents of the Frazer-Tylor school of religion to be the desire to placate the ghosts of the dead and to ensure the kindly offices of such spirits as could influence the fate of men. It is probable that all gifts which found their way to the altar were partly of this type, since, for instance, the paying of tribute can scarcely be separated from the desire to propitiate the one who receives the tribute. This element in gift-sacrifices is preserved in the Hebrew phrase *riach-nichoach* (a smell of appeasement, a soothing, tranquillizing odour).

The second main aspect involved in sacrifice is expiation. The aim is to get rid of sin. Such ideas probably lie behind the whole sacrificial system of post-exilic times. But properly, in post-exilic times, there were two expiatory 'sacrifices', though it is misleading to attach the word 'sacrifice' to them. These two offerings were the *chattath* ('sin-offering') and the *'asham* ('guilt-offering').

The sin-offering dealt with minor offences (Leviticus 5.1-6), with ceremonial uncleanness, and with unintentional (mostly ritual) offences. The fat portions and certain selected portions of the animal which had been brought as a sin-offering, were consumed on the altar; this was the rule followed in all cases, but the remainder (i.e. the carcase as a whole) went nowhere near the altar. In the case of offences in which the people as a whole were involved or in which a priest was involved, the carcase had to be taken outside the camp with the skin and entrails, and there burnt. In cases where the priest was not personally involved in the error, the carcase was eaten by the priests. But the main point of the *chattath* ('sin-offering') was that, apart from those select portions which were always given to God and burned up in smoke on the altar, the animal was removed from sight, taken away. With it, it was believed, the sin was taken away and removed. It was covered, or 'wiped away', to use the latest explanation of the word *kipper* ('atone'), and thus no longer could lie between man and God. The same ritual applied to the *'asham* ('guilt-offering'), except that the *'asham* dealt with offences where the damage could be assessed.

The third aspect of sacrificial offerings is that of communion. It was formerly the custom to think of the *zebach* ('sacrifice') as belonging to this type of offering. This offering was eaten by the worshippers, apart, that is, from the fat and such select portions as were burned on the altar for the Deity, whatever the type of offering. The late Professor W. Robertson Smith saw in this sacred meal support for his theory that the origin of religion was to be found in totemism. He noted that part of the beast was burned on the altar and the rest eaten by the worshippers, and saw here evidence of a common meal in which God and people met together, ate together, and thus strengthened the common 'family' bonds which at one time were centred in the totem. But, as we have seen, the fact that certain portions were burned on the altar is not due to the fact that the offering is a *zebach* and so the basis of a common meal. Those particular portions were burnt on the altar in any case. It is much more likely that the beast having been consecrated by the priest and made 'holy' was regarded as being holy food, so that the worshippers in partaking of it, partook of the life of the God, and were thus ensured well-being and continued prosperity. This offering was sometimes called a *shelem*, whence the translation 'peace-offering'. The explanation formerly given was that this ensured peaceful relations with God, and thus the meal was a survival of totemistic beliefs. It is more probable, however, that we should think of 'peace-offering' in the sense of 'health-offering', since the word *shalom* means not only 'peace', but 'health', 'prosperity', and all such kindred ideas. Thus the *zebach-shelem* was an offering which, being eaten by the worshippers, ensured continued health and well-being.

There remains one other animal which was slaughtered ritually in Old Testament times, and still is slaughtered in connection with the same ritual to this day. We refer to the Passover Lamb. The ritual of the Passover Lamb is wholly different from all other rituals. It never was a temple ritual, but always essentially a home rite. This is why the rite could still be observed after the destruction of the temple. In the time of our Lord, the passover lambs were slain in the temple, and the blood was passed up along a line of priests to be cast at the foot of the altar, but everything else in the Passover rite proper belonged to the home. The rite was originally an apotropaic rite, that is, a rite for the turning away of evil spirits. It was adapted by the Hebrews and associated with the great deliverance from Egypt, so that it became a symbol of salvation, a continual memorial of that mighty act of salvation whereby God brought Israel out of Egypt to be a people specially chosen and called by Him. There was never any sense in which the Passover Lamb could be a gift to God; there was never any sense in which it could be regarded as expiatory; there was never any sense in which it could be thought of as a communion-offering. It was always, in Old Testament times, and still is, the observance of the LORD'S passover, when He passed over the houses of the Israelites, smote the Egyptians and released His people from the 'house of bondmen'.

When we turn to the New Testament, what does the

word 'sacrifice' mean? The answer is that it means different things at different times, and that each instance must be judged separately.

To take the various occurrences in turn, we have first the two passages in the Gospel according to St. Matthew where the passage from Hosea (6.6) is quoted. These are Matthew 9.13 and 12.7. In the former of these Jesus is attacking the ritual rules of cleanness which loomed so largely in the Judaism of the time. He had been sitting at meat with 'publicans and sinners', people who were not ritually clean. The Pharisees objected, and Jesus bade them go and learn the meaning of Hosea 6.6. It was part of the general attack which Jesus made on the official religion of the day with all its minute regulations. It was an attack on the whole principle of Habdalah, that system of separation between clean and unclean, holy and common, which was the foundation of Judaism. The second case (Matthew 12.7) is the spearhead of another attack on the official religion of the day, once more against the principle of Habdalah as it was applied to the separation of the Sabbath from the rest of the days. In both cases Hosea 6.6 is used in an attack on ritualistic practices in daily life as being of first importance. The claim of Jesus was that 'mercy' comes first, and that no so-called religious rules were legitimate when they were used to keep sinners out.

In the Gospel according to St. Mark there are two instances of the use of the word 'sacrifice'. One is a reference (Mark 9.49, but only in the Western text) to the custom of sprinkling salt on the cereal-offerings of the post-exilic period (Leviticus 2.13). The other (12.33) is the famous case of the scribe whom Jesus declared to be not far from the Kingdom of God, because he knew that loving God with the whole self and loving one's neighbour as one's self is worth more than the whole sum total of all ritual offerings of every type.

The two references in the Gospel according to St. Luke (2.24 and 13.1) are direct references to offerings that were brought to the temple. The former concerned the pre-scribed gifts brought by the mother at the presentation of the first-born; the second refers to Pilate having mixed the blood of men with the blood of the sacrifices. The two cases in Acts (7.41 and 7.42) are of the same type, the first referring to the offerings (*zebach*) which provided the sacred meal in the cult of the Golden Calf, and the other being a quotation from Amos 5.25, where the passage is made to refer to the illegitimate rites of the Golden Calf.

In the Epistles the references are more complicated and far from easy of precise explanation. The various strands and intentions become interwoven, just as, indeed, already is the case in Leviticus 1.4, where even the burnt-offering (the gift to God wholly burned on the altar) is spoken of as being 'accepted for him (the giver) to make atonement (i.e. *kipper*, wipe away sin) for him', and as being burned on the altar as 'a sweet savour (appeasing odour) unto the Lord' (1.9). Here we get a suggestion of placating God, an idea which, as we have already pointed out, is in prac-tice inseparable from the idea of a tribute-gift. Thus in Romans 12.1, the brethren are bidden to 'present (their) bodies a living sacrifice, holy, acceptable (well-pleasing) to God'. The Greek word translated 'sacrifice' is *thusia*, which properly means an animal that is slain. The extent to which these 'sacrificial' words can vary from their original meaning is illustrated by the phrase 'living sacri-fice'. From the strictly etymological view, 'living' is the one thing which a *thusia* could not be when presented to the Deity. The most likely meaning of the word 'sacrifice' here is 'gift'. We are to present our bodies wholly to God, recognizing that they are to be entirely His. At the same time, such a gift is realized to be 'acceptable, well-pleasing' to Him. Here we have to decide whether we mean 'please' or 'placate'. The same double association is to be found in Ephesians 5.2, where the writer speaks of Christ, who 'gave himself up for us, an offering and a sacrifice to God for an odour of a sweet smell'. Here we have the idea of a gift and the idea of pleasing God. There is another element, namely that it was 'for us', which may possibly mean 'instead of', but more likely means 'on behalf of'. This latter is the meaning in such passages as Leviticus 1.4: 'it shall be accepted *for him* to make atonement for him'. This is not to deny the idea of substitution in connection with the sacrifice of Christ, but only to deny that it is involved together with the idea of a gift to God. The reference in Philippians 4.18 is a comparison between the gifts brought to Paul by Epaphroditus and 'an odour of sweet smell, a sacrifice acceptable, well-pleasing to God'. This passage is valuable in that it shows that the phrase 'sacrifice acceptable . . .' signifies a gift that gives great pleasure to the recipient. Presumably this was the main meaning Paul attached to the phrase regularly, and this is why the comparison came into his mind on this occasion. Paul's gratefulness to the Philippian Christians shines out through the whole letter, wrapped up as it is with his great delight that the seed he had sown bore such grateful fruit. The reference in I Corinthians 10.18 is 'behold Israel after the flesh: have not they which eat the sacrifices communion (*koinonia*) with the altar?' This apparently refers to the Jewish *zebach*, that sacrifice which was eaten by the worshipper (apart, that is, from those select pieces which were burned on the altar, whatever the animal that was slain), so that 'communion with the altar' means that in the sacred meal, the eaters came to be 'in communion with' Christ. Paul is drawing an analogy between the eating of the *zebach* and the sacred meals both of the Christians and of the idolators of Corinth. The one is the 'communion (*koinonia*) of the body and blood of Christ' (verse 16) and the other is the 'communion of devils' (verse 20). The point is, apparently, not that those who partake of the sacred meal are bound together into a communion but that those who partake are bound into a communion with Christ. They eat of Him, just as the Jews partook of holy food. Modern Christians 'eat His body' and 'drink His blood'. Some hold that they partake of the actual body in or with the elements; others hold that they eat by faith, and that the elements are not in any sense His body and blood. By faith we are partakers of the Nature of Christ.

The references to the sacrificial system in the Epistle to the Hebrews are most confused and confusing, so much so that it is difficult to use the Old Testament sacrificial system in order to explain what the writer of the epistle means. In Hebrew 5.1 we have an admirable example of the confusion which creeps in when men speak of 'sacrifice'. The writer is apparently quoting the Septuagint (Codex A) of I Kings 8.64 with its 'gifts and sacrifices', but he adds 'for sins'. It seems to be the case that the original text of Hebrew 5.1 distinguished between 'gifts' and 'sacrifices for sins', though this is not wholly certain. What is certain is that the omission at an early date (see Codex B, etc.) of the particle *te* makes both the gifts and the sacrifices to be 'for sins'. Thus, possibly in the original text of Hebrew 5.1, and certainly in the B-text, the whole sacrificial system is regarded as having as its object the removal of sin.

The same kind of confusion is found in Hebrew 7.27, where the writer says that the high-priest daily offered up 'sacrifices, first for his own sins, and then for the sins of the people'. This is not an accurate statement. The Hebrew text of Leviticus 6.13 (EVV, 20) and the Septuagint text also are uncertain as to whether the high-priest offered the cereal-offering morning and evening on the day of his anointing only or every day (Hebrew *tamid*, Greek *dia pantos*, English *perpetually*). We do know, however, that in the last days of the Temple, the high-priest did in fact offer these sacrifices every day, and Philo bears this testimony also. The sacrifices actually were cereal-offerings, but Septuagint calls them *thusia*, so that here the writer to the Hebrews is assuming that all sacrifices of whatever kind were for sins. This idea is carried forward in Hebrews 9.26 and applied to the sacrifice of Jesus, which was (he says) to put away sin. This is the writer's general and regular application of the meaning of Old Testament sacrifices to the sacrifice of Christ. It was 'for sins', 'to put away sins'. He regards the whole sacrificial system in general as having its object the putting away of sins.

In the New Testament, then, the sacrifice of Christ is a gift to God, it is for us, and it is for putting away sin. Can it be to placate God? If so, then we have the idea of an angry God who requires a gift, and further, requires the gift of a bloody sacrifice, before He is willing to forgive man his sin. When the writer of Hebrews 9.22 says that 'apart from shedding of blood there is no remission' of sin, is he right? His statement is not exactly this, because he prefaces it by saying, 'according to the law'. His whole argument is on the basis of the Jewish law, particularly, if not indeed wholly, in its ritual aspects. But to those who think in terms of Hosea 6.6 and Mark 12.33, this argument from the law is not impressive, though they would be prepared to accept the interpretation that without sacrifice (surrender, self-giving) there is no remission of sins. This is because there must be full repentance and full self-surrender on the part of the sinner. It is impossible to think that God needs to change His mind in any way in order to forgive men. Whatever change takes place, must take place in the sinner. He must turn back to God; he must repent. The gift that he must bring is himself, nothing less than this. He must give his all, himself, everything. All this he must give in humble repentance and true faith. God does not require from man a full penitence in the absolute sense. He requires from man a full penitence, all of which he is capable. It is the greatest saint who is the most penitent, and our penitence grows with the years. The gift-sacrifice which we bring to God is ourselves. And yet not only for ourselves, because we are not by any means isolated individuals. In our surrender to God, we give ourselves not only for ourselves, but for our 'neighbour', since we are bound indissolubly with him. And our 'neighbour' is every man. It is in this sense that the sacrifice of Christ, Christ's gift of Himself, is for us. It is instead of us, that is, instead of the whole race of man. But it is not instead of us in the sense that His sacrifice avails for me apart from any self-giving of mine. It is for me, because He gave Himself as a man, sharer in our common woe, sharer in the travail to which we are all born because of the sins of mankind. It is in this way that the death of Christ—His self-giving—is representative.

But what about the removal of sin? The analogy for this in the Old Testament is the sin-offering. This sin-offering was not in any sense a gift to God, since it was never taken to the altar, that is, apart from those select portions which were consumed on the altar as a matter of course, whatever the nature of the sacrificial-beast. The writer of the Epistle to the Hebrews makes the most of this sin-offering with the taking of the slain beast away ' outside the camp ', even to drawing an analogy between that rite and the fact that Jesus was crucified ' outside Jerusalem '. We have written concerning this aspect of the death of Christ in a previous book, *I Believe In* (pp. 67-70). The context there is a discussion of II Corinthians 5.21, which we claimed should read ' Him who knew no sin he made to be a sin-offering on our behalf '. Just as the sin-offering was taken away from between the sinner and the altar, so Christ takes away our sin so that it no longer stands between us and God, preventing at-one-ment of God and man. The analogy, however, is far from complete, because the sin-offerings of the Old Testament did not deal with deliberate sin, sin ' with a high hand ', as the phrase goes. They dealt almost wholly with accidental ritual offences, and the Rabbis could say ' sin-offering and guilt-offering effect atonement ', but that Death and the Day of Atonement atone with repentance (Mishna, *Yoma* 7.5).

We must, nevertheless, beware of falling into the snare of which the prophets were always warning men, namely, the belief that sacrifices themselves are effectual. The sacrifices of the Temple were not in themselves effective, and neither is the death of Christ. There must also be repentance. There is no forgiveness without sacrifice, but equally there is no forgiveness without repentance.

There is another sacrificial reference to the death of Christ, namely I Corinthians 5.7: 'Christ our passover is sacrificed for us.' Here there is no question of any gift to God, nor, to the first degree, at any rate, any question of the removal of sin. As we have pointed out, the Passover ritual is wholly different from other sacrificial rites. The slaying of the Passover Lamb is the commemoration of the great salvation which God wrought for Israel. Thus, the phrase 'Christ our Passover' means Christ our Saviour.

INDEX OF SUBJECTS

ADAD-NIRARI III, 12
Albright, W. F., 13
Altar, 93
Amos and Hosea (similarities), 40-51
Amos and Hosea (differences), 51f.
Ancient logic, 16
Assyrian wars, 13
Athanasius, 23
Atonement, 114

BAAL, 56f.

CAIN and Abel, 94
Chesed, 45, 70, 80ff.
Chosen people, 40ff.
Chronology of kings, 12
Communion-sacrifices, 111, 116
Covenant, 55
Cultic prophets, 9f., 16

DAY of Atonement, 119
Deuteronomic reforms, 22
Dikaiosune, 73ff.

EARTHQUAKE (Uzziah), 11f.
Ecstasy, 16-19
Election, 44
Engnell, I., 11

FEASTS, 91

GIFT-SACRIFICES, 106ff., 116, 118
Grace, 45

Guilt-offering, 59, 110

HABDALAH, 113
Henotheism, 19
Holiness, 95
Holy Spirit, 20, 87

INHUMAN conduct, 47
Islam, 46

JEREMIAH, call, etc., 21-24
Jeroboam II, 11f.
Jerome, 10
Jezreel, 35, 58
Johnson, A. R., 16

KARKAR, 13
Knowledge of God, 49
Koinonia, 115

LÉVY-BRUHL, M., 16
Lo-'ammi, 36, 48
Lo-ruhamah, 37
Low gods, 94

MAGIC, 33
Messianism, 58
Mishpat, 70, 76ff., 85
Morality, 52
Mount of God, 61
Mowinckel, S., 28f., 32
Muhammad, 20

Nabi', 16f., 18

New covenant, 85
New Israel, 50
Numinous, 17f., 105f.

OTTO, R., 17f., 105f.

PASSOVER, 92f., 112f., 120
Peace-offerings, 111
Penalty for sin, 45, 49, 60
Personal experience of God, 25, 40
Pre-logical thought, 16
Prophet (cult), 9f., 16
Prophet (test), 10ff.
Prophets and sacrifice, 89

Qodesh, 95, 105
Qur'an, 20

Rachamim, 83f.
Ras Shamra, 9
Rejection of Israel, 42
Robinson, H. W., 33
Robinson, T. H., 28
Ruach, 84f.

SACRED lot, 17
Sacrifice (meaning of word), 103f.
Sacrifice (Amos), 89-94, 95
Sacrifice (Ezekiel), 100
Sacrifice (Hosea), 97f.
Sacrifice (Isaiah), 95f.
Sacrifice (Jeremiah), 89-91, 95, 98f.
Sacrifice (types), 89f.

Sacrifice of Christ, 117f.
Sanday and Headlam, 74
Satan, 20
Saviour-God, 53, 55
Scythians, 21
Septuagint, 10, 57, 63f., 80, 116
Shalmaneser III, 13
Shema', 66
Sin and suffering, 60
Sin-offerings, 59, 110, 119
Sub-conscious, 17
Symbolic actions, 33

TEN Commandments, 54, 66
Thiele, E. R., 12
Tiglath-pileser III, 13
Totemism, 111
Tsedaqah, 70, 71ff.
Types of prophecy, 28, 32

UGARIT, 9

VALUES, 38
Vulgate, 10, 81

WILDERNESS-MOTIF, 43, 56
Witness of Spirit, 18, 23ff.
Word of God, 43, 56

Yada' (know), 62

ZADOKITES, 22, 99

INDEX OF BIBLICAL REFERENCES

GENESIS
    4.1 : 62
    4.3-5 : 94f.
    4.13 : 60
    4.26 : 43
    38.2 : 43
    38.26 : 71
    48.22 : 41

EXODUS
    3.12 : 43
    6.3 : 43
    13.11-13 : 95
    13.25 : 95
    20 : 54f., 66, 67
    23.14-16 : 92
    34.19f. : 95

LEVITICUS
    1.4 : 114, 115
    1.9 : 114
    2.13 : 113
    3.1-17 : 89f.
    5.1-6 : 110
    6.20 : 117
    18.18 : 31
    19.18 : 67, 88
    23 : 92

NUMBERS
    5.14, 30 : 84
    8.8-32 : 107

DEUTERONOMY
    5.6-21 : 66, 67
    6.4-5 : 66, 88
    12.15f. : 94
    12.20-28 : 90
    13.2-3 : 19
    16.3 : 91
    16.13-17 : 91
    18.22 : 19
    21.15-17 : 31
    23.19 : 71
    24.13 : 75f.
    25.15 : 71
    32.10ff. : 43
    34.10 : 44

JOSHUA
    7.24, 26 : 56

JUDGES
    13.25 : 86
    14.6, 19 : 86
    15.14 : 86

I SAMUEL
    2.27f. : 22, 99
    6.3, 4, 8, 17 : 59
    9.10 : 78
    10.5-13 : 16
    10.6, 10, 11 : 86
    12.12 : 77
    14.34 : 93
    16.7 : 79

I SAMUEL—*cont.*
19.18-24 : 16
28.16 : 60

II SAMUEL
21.17 : 36
24.1, 17 : 20

I KINGS
4.21 : 90
8.64 : 116
11.36 : 36
15.4 : 36
22.19-24 : 19

II KINGS
9.11 : 16
9.24, 27, 33 : 36
10.14 : 36
10.15-26 : 36
12.17 : 59
19.35f. : 38
22.14-20 : 78
23.9 : 99

I CHRONICLES
21.1 : 20

NEHEMIAH
8.13-17 : 92
9.20 : 87

PSALMS
2.2, 3 : 61
4.5 : 71
40.10 : 71
51.19 : 71
103.6 : 75
103.13, 14 : 83
132.9 : 71
146.5-16 : 75

ISAIAH
1.11-15 : 95f.
1.17 : 101

ISAIAH—*cont.*
5.18 : 60
6.1-6 : 97
6.4 : 12, 96
6.5 : 96
6.9-12 : 30
6.12 : 50
7.3 : 35, 49
8.11-18 : 35
11.4 : 74
20.2 : 33
30.16 : 15
37.36 : 38
40-55 : 44
40-66 : 71
40.2 : 60
40.6 : 80, 81
41.2 : 71
41.10 : 71
45.8 : 71
53 : 60
53.1 : 61
53.5, 6, 10 : 59
53.12 : 60
62.1 : 71
63.7-14 : 44

JEREMIAH
1 : 21
1.1 : 99
1.5 : 21
2.2 : 30, 56, 81
7.4 : 99
7.11 : 99
7.14, 20 : 99
7.21 : 98
7.22 : 89, 98
8.4-7 : 85
8.7f. : 22, 78, 79
11.1-8 : 22
11.21-23 : 22
13 : 34
19.12 : 99
20.7 : 20
20.7-9 : 22

JEREMIAH—*cont.*
25.17 : 34
29.26 : 16
31.20 : 24
31.32 : 81
31.31-34 : 82, 85
44.16-19, 21 : 9
49.29 : 37

LAMENTATIONS
3.39 : 60

EZEKIEL
1.3 : 100
8 : 100
16.1-34 : 34
40-48 : 78, 100
46.2 : 78

DANIEL
4.27 : 75
8.12, 13 : 60
9.24 : 60

HOSEA
1-3 : 14
1 : 9, 27, 30, 31, 33, 37
1.10 : 10
1.2-9 : 27, 51
1.2 : 10, 11, 30, 97
1.4 : 37, 51, 58
1.6 : 37, 51, 81, 82
1.7 : 28, 29, 32, 37
1.9 : 37, 48, 51, 58
1.10-2.23 : 27
1.10-2.1 : 32, 50
2.2-23 : 28f., 30, 31, 48
2.2 : 29, 55
2.4 : 82
2.6, 7 : 56
2.12 : 14
2.15-23 : 51
2.15 : 29, 30, 42, 56, 57, 70, 83

HOSEA—*cont.*
2.16 : 33
2.19 : 70, 80, 81, 83, 85
2.23 : 58
3 : 27-33, 97
3.1-5 : 27, 50
3.3 : 15
3.4 : 50, 97
3.5 : 14, 50
4.2 : 49, 100
4.3 : 48
4.5-11 : 100
4.6 : 49
4.12 : 84, 85
4.19 : 49
5.1-4, 119
5.4 : 83, 84
5.13 : 61
5.15 : 58, 59, 61, 62
6.1-3 : 14, 61
6.2 : 15, 62
6.4-11 : 49
6.6 : 7, 81, 88, 97, 113
7 : 49
8 : 49
8.13 : 98
9 : 49
9.4 : 98
9.10 : 42
10 : 49
11 : 64f.
11.1-11 : 63
11.1-2 : 49
11.1 : 44
11.5 : 65
11.7 : 83, 85
11.8-9 : 14
11.10, 11 : 15, 51, 65
12.13 : 44
13.4 : 44
13.14 : 51
14 : 15, 51, 63
14.2 : 63
14.5, 6 : 63

AMOS
  1.1 : 12
  1.2 : 48
  1.3-5 : 36
  2.6 : 74
  2.9-10 : 40, 41
  2.11-12 : 42
  3.2 : 42, 62
  5.25 : 30, 89, 115
  7.7-9 : 47
  7.10 : 11
  7.14 : 9, 18
  8.1-2 : 47
  8.9 : 11
  8.14 : 47
  9.7 : 37, 42
  9.8 : 45
  9.11-15 : 45

MICAH
  3.8 : 86
  6.8 : 81, 97

ZECHARIAH
  4.6 : 38
  11.8 : 34
  13.4 : 18
  14.5 : 12

MATTHEW
  3.10 : 46
  6.1 : 75
  7.11 : 56
  9.13 : 88, 113
  12.7 : 88, 113

MARK
  9.49 : 113

MARK—cont.
  12.28-34 : 66
  12.33 : 89, 113

LUKE
  2.24 : 114
  4.24 : 20
  13.1 : 114
  13.6-8 : 46
  13.34 : 20
  16.31 : 20

ACTS
  7.41f. : 114

I CORINTHIANS
  5.7 : 120
  10.16, 18, 20 : 115
  12 : 19
  13 : 19

II CORINTHIANS
  5.21 : 119

EPHESIANS
  5.2 : 115

PHILIPPIANS
  4.18 : 115

HEBREWS
  5.1 : 116
  7.27 : 117
  9.22, 26 : 117

I JOHN
  5.3 : 67